DATE DUE

BIZARRE SEX LAWS

Bizarre Sex Laws

AN AROUND-THE-WORLD PEEK INTO
THE STRANGE AND UNEXPECTED

Gregory LaFarge

imagine!
Publishing

An Imagine Book

Published by Charlesbridge

85 Main Street, Watertown, MA 02472

(617) 926-0329

www.charlesbridge.com

Library of Congress Cataloging-in-Publication Data
LaFarge, Gregory.
  Bizarre sex laws : an around-the-world peek into the strange and unexpected /
Gregory LaFarge.
     p. cm.
  "An Imagine Book."
  ISBN 978-1-936140-25-1
1. Sex and law—Humor. 2. Sex and law—Miscellanea. 3. Sex and law—Humor—
United States. 4. Sex and law—Miscellanea—United States. 5. Sex—Humor.
I. Title.
  K5194.L34 2011
  345'.0253--dc22

                    2010048023

2 4 6 8 10 9 7 5 3 1

For information about custom editions, special sales,

premium and corporate purchases, please contact

Charlesbridge Publishing at specialsales@charlesbridge.com

contents

Introduction

In the 1989 Woody Allen movie *Crimes and Misdemeanors*, Allen's character Clifford Stern struggles to respond when his visibly distraught sister tells him of a date gone wrong. It seemed to be going fine, Barbara reports, but the evening ended with the man "going to the bathroom" on her in bed. When Clifford's wife asks him why this happened, the only explanation he can come up with is that "human sexuality is a strange thing."

For centuries, lawmakers have struggled with this conundrum. One person's sexual urges may seem repulsive or lewd to others, one culture's sexual mores immoral and obscene to a different population. Who decides what's acceptable and what's not? What's private and what's suitable for public consumption? What behavior is a decision between two people and what's a cultural norm?

As far back as written records exist, there are laws governing sexual conduct. In the beginning, there was no distinction between religious law and civil law, so holy books established acceptable (and required) sexual behavior. Even today, the Torah, the Qur'an, the Bible, and other scriptures are the basis for sex laws in most of the world. But attitudes have shifted with each successive civilization and generation, and the law reflects that. What was normal and acceptable for ancient Greeks can seem by turns odd or strangely progressive by modern standards. Victorians were notoriously prudish, but in some respects they accepted behavior that's frowned upon today.

Sex laws tend to reflect society's morals, but sometimes there's a lag time between the fast-paced world and the slow and steady pace of the legal system. Some laws on the books today date back centuries, and lawmakers are constantly challenged to create new laws or update the old ones to reflect current-day realities. There may be no need to regulate behavior around steamship landings as one Massachusetts law does, but there's an increasing need to address the problem of online sexual predators.

And then there's the issue of privacy. Sex is a fundamentally private act, so who decides where to draw the line about what can go on behind closed doors? Is it an individual or a legal decision? The balance between protecting individual liberties and protecting individuals from harm (or "eroding public morals") is constantly in play in laws regarding sex, and some cultures value individual liberty more than others.

In this book, we'll look at the many different ways sexuality is regulated around the world and take a peek back in time to see the way our predecessors legislated it. From laws regulating sex as a commodity to those regarding if, when, and where (and with what) you can masturbate, there are statutes that will shock you, amuse you, puzzle you, and possibly apply to you. And along with learning about the laws, you'll hear about the myriad and often bizarre ways in which people break them. For every person who stays within the law, there are dozens of others who find new and unique ways to test the limits and give lawmakers something new to interpret.

You may be surprised to find that you've been breaking the law for years without even knowing it. And you will definitely be surprised to find out the ways that some of your fellow citizens are ending up behind bars. While some laws may seem silly and archaic to you, at some point in time our current laws may seem the same way. And for those laws that seem overly progressive, it may just be that the place where you live hasn't quite caught up yet.

Sex is a sensitive subject no matter what. But looking at it through the (hopefully) objective eye of the law takes some of the emotion out of it and allows us to consider it for what it really is: a human behavior that is sometimes inexplicable, but always endlessly interesting.

The World's Oldest Profession

Whether you call them hookers, streetwalkers, call girls, or ladies of the night, those who sell sex for a living have been around since the beginning of written history. Prostitution laws are some of the most complicated, ignored, and unevenly enforced sex laws there are, and they vary wildly even within a single country. The only thing that stays the same across the board is that there is always a high demand for the services being offered.

Love for Sale: Can It Land You in Jail?

Prostitution is legal in seventy-seven countries. It is legally restricted in eleven countries, and illegal in 109 countries. Five countries have no laws regarding prostitution: Bulgaria, Guinea-Bissau, Lesotho, Mozambique, and Indonesia, where it is technically outlawed under Islamic law because it's an immoral behavior.

Prostitution is legal in **Mexico**, but pimping and prostitution of minors under eighteen is against the law.

In **Thailand**, prostitution is against the law, but the country has one of the most (if not *the* most) active sex tourism industries in the world and is known for forced prostitution of children.

In **Malaysia**, public solicitation of a prostitute is illegal, but there are no laws governing private solicitation.

In **Armenia**, prostitution and sex tourism are legal, but it's illegal to pimp or run a brothel.

In **Bolivia**, women over eighteen can legally pursue prostitution as a career. In **Cuba**, the legal age is seventeen.

Prostitution is legal in **Lebanon** if a brothel permit is secured, but officials report that no one has applied for a permit since the 1970s. Instead, most would-be clients go to "super nightclubs" where they can sit next to women, kiss, and engage in "light petting" (anything further is illegal in such a club). If the "artist" (i.e. prostitute) in the club agrees to a "date" within the next seven days, sex is considered to be part of the deal and money will then change hands.

In **Latvia**, prostitution is legal, but prostitutes must have a monthly health check. In Panama, prostitutes are supposed to register and carry ID cards, but few ever do.

In **Senegal**, prostitution is legal for those over the age of twenty-one who register with the police, carry a valid sanitary card, and test negative for sexually transmitted infections.

In **Japan**, prostitution is illegal, but that only includes acts of intercourse. Other sex acts, such as oral sex and erotic massage, are considered legal for purchase and often take place legally in sex clubs.

In **India**, prostitution is legal, but it's illegal to advertise it. Pimping and procuring prostitutes is illegal. It's also illegal to advertise prostitution in **Moldova**, but the penalty for doing so is only a small fine.

After the Cultural Revolution in **China**, prostitution was criminalized and prostitutes who were caught were shackled and led through the streets in "shame parades." Those found guilty of the offense of prostitution are now given a first-time fine of around $800 and a two-week stay in jail. In the past, the names of both the prostitute and her client were often printed and displayed in public. In 2010, the Chinese government finally abolished the practice of shame parades. The number of male prostitutes (called "ducks") in China has risen in recent years.

In the **Democratic Republic of Congo**, forced prostitution and prostitution under the age of eighteen are illegal. Forced prostitution is illegal in **Nepal**, but prostitution by choice is not.

In **Norway**, buying (not selling) sex is now against the law. If caught purchasing sex either in Norway or in another country, Norwegian citizens face a steep fine and/or a six-month jail sentence which is extended to three years if the person from whom the sex is purchased is underage. The aim of the law is to combat not only prostitution but sex tourism, which is why the prostitutes themselves are not arrested in the transaction. As part of the new regulation, lawmakers

developed a budget to offer Norwegian prostitutes free health care, drug and alcohol treatment, and education to get them out of the world's oldest profession.

In **Sweden**, a similar law recently passed: Selling sex is legal, but buying it isn't. "Brokering" it (pimping) also now carries a stiffer penalty. Those caught pimping can be sentenced to anywhere from six months to ten years in prison. Law enforcement officials say that it's hard to prove the crime has taken place unless the john is caught in the act. Since the law was enacted, the number of johns arrested has increased by 100 percent.

In 2010, **Iceland** passed a law outlawing the purchase of sex.

Prostitution is legal in **Denmark**. Danish sex workers made international headlines during the 2010 Climate Change conference in Copenhagen when they offered their services for free to those who came to town to combat global warming.

Prostitution is legal in **Canada**, but brothels, pimping, and forced and underage prostitution are prohibited.

Prostitution was outlawed in the state of **Rhode Island** only in 2009. Until that time, there was no law specifically dealing with it even though pimping, street solicitation, and running a brothel were illegal.

In the **UK**, "kerb crawling" or street solicitation is illegal, but other forms of prostitution are not. It's also illegal to purchase sex from a prostitute who is under force, and ignorance of the fact is not an excuse.

Double Standards

In **Bangladesh**, female prostitution is legal, but male prostitution isn't.

In **Brazil**, female prostitution is illegal but typically ignored, but transvestite prostitutes are usually arrested for "offending public morals."

"Beach gigolos" in **Indonesia** have recently become the target of law enforcement officials. The men, who frequent local beaches looking for rich foreign women on holiday, had become a fixture on the island of Bali, approaching and romancing older women in exchange for gifts. To crack down on the gigolos, police went looking for tan, muscular men, and arrested twenty-eight of them in a raid. The men claimed to be surf instructors and were later released.

Call Me

While selling sex on the street is illegal in many places, sometimes it's legal to arrange for paid sex over the phone. In the **United States**, escort services are legal and a fee may be paid as long as it is only for "companionship" (i.e. sex doesn't take place). An escort may of her own will decide to have sex with the client in an agreement outside of the paid agreement.

In **California**, escort services must be licensed. In **Utah**, they are taxed if nudity appears in their advertising.

The Land Down Under

In **Australia**, prostitution laws vary by territory. It's legal in **Queensland**. In **South Australia**, it's only illegal to earn money through prostitution. In **Western Australia**, you can earn money through prostitution, but you have to pay taxes on it and submit to periodic health exams. Brothels are allowed in the city of **Melbourne**, but in other parts of **Victoria**, they can't be situated within one hundred meters of a dwelling or two hundred meters of a church, hospital, or any other place where children are likely to be.

The Wild West

Nevada is the only state in the United States that allows legal prostitution in regulated brothels in eleven rural counties. Condoms are required and all customers are required to be serviced. Prostitutes are considered independent contractors and can set their own rates and list of services. Prostitution outside a brothel is considered a misdemeanor, and fines run up to $1,000.

In 2010, a man became the first legal gigolo in the state of Nevada. The man, whom some called "the prostidude," quit his job after two months (and ten customers) to return to acting in porn films.

Houses of Ill Repute

Brothels have been illegal in **France** since 1946, but in 2010 a female member of Parliament called for them to be reinstated, citing safety issues for street prostitutes as an issue.

In **Hong Kong**, there were once over two hundred brothels and seven thousand licensed prostitutes. Prostitution was outlawed in 1932. It's now legal again, but "vice houses" (brothels) are not.

In **Tunisia**, there are government-sanctioned brothels that are legal to visit.

Brothels are legal in **Switzerland**, and the country's first gay brothel opened in 2009.

Brothels are legal in the **Czech Republic**. One Czech brothel even offers sex for free as long as the clients are willing to be webcasted in the act (the brothel owners are paid by those who watch online).

In the **UK**, single-woman brothels are legal, but in order to make it safer for women, the government is considering a law which would allow small-scale brothels staffed by up to two prostitutes and a receptionist or maid.

Brothels are legal in **Germany**, but lawmakers balked at "recession-busting" techniques introduced by some brothels in 2009: "flat-rate sex," modeled on all-you-can-eat promotions at restaurants. Out-raged lawmakers focused immigration and hygiene raids on brothels that advertised them.

There's a popular Internet urban legend that sororities houses in the **United States** are technically illegal in certain states because more than three unmarried women living together in a house would be considered a brothel. In fact, such laws never existed because brothels are recognized not by the gender of the inhabitants of a house, but rather by the activities they engaged in.

Spa Time?

In countries in which brothels are illegal, massage parlors, saunas, or "Asian spas" are often cover operations for prostitution. In the **United States**, massage parlors are the frequent target of raids and sting operations.

Massage parlors are against the law in **Dubai**. In **England**, they're legal, but it's illegal to advertise them.

Those who have prior convictions of prostitution are ineligible to be licensed as massage therapists in **Louisiana**.

Legal Tender

What passes as prostitution can vary from place to place. A woman in **Oklahoma** was arrested for prostitution for offering oral sex in exchange for a box of Fritos. The box was valued at $30 and the woman's fine came to over $1,000.

A baseball fan was arrested for offering sex in exchange for tickets to see the **Philadelphia** Phillies in the World Series in 2009. Police tracked the woman through an ad that she posted on the free classified ads site Craigslist. An undercover male police officer went to meet her, and the woman offered to perform sex acts on the man and his brother in exchange for tickets to the sold-out game.

The online classified service Craigslist became a target for police after ads in its "adult services" section resulted in several murders. In 2010, Craigslist shut down its adult services section permanently.

A **Brooklyn**, New York, detective was arrested for offering lighter sentencing to three accused drug dealers in exchange for sex.

An **Arizona** tattoo artist was charged with sexual misconduct with a minor after offering to give a girl a tattoo in exchange for sex. In that state, it's illegal for a minor to get a tattoo without the presence of a parent or guardian, so when the underage girl requested one, the tattoo artist suggested that he would do it if the girl would have sex with him.

A guard on the border between the **United States** and **Mexico** was arrested for offering Mexican women illegal entrance into the United States in exchange for sex. In **California**, a highway patrolman was found guilty of soliciting sex in exchange for fixing a speeding ticket.

A dentist in **North Carolina** was charged with writing false prescriptions in exchange for sex. Before being tried, the man was found murdered. Those for whom he had been writing prescriptions stand accused.

Two **Tennessee** women were arrested for offering sex in exchange for cigarettes.

Putting on the Red Light

Dating back to the nineteenth century, areas where prostitution is legal are often called "red-light districts" because street lamps with red bulbs were used to mark the boundaries of the zones. There are twelve red-light districts in the **Netherlands** and several in Germany.

Patpong in **Bangkok** was considered the world's most famous red-light district, but it has largely been replaced by **Sukhumvit**. Legal prostitution and sex-related services take place in these areas, but they have also become notorious for the illegal sex trade, involving thousands of underage girls.

In **Singapore**, prostitution is legal in a red-light district as long as prostitutes submit to mandatory health checks.

In **France**, standing on a street corner where prostitutes are known to hang out and wearing revealing clothing is considered to be "passive solicitation" and is subject to a fine. The first women arrested on this charge were cleared in court.

Power in the Union

In some countries where prostitution is legal there are sex workers unions, which generally represent prostitutes, strippers, nude models, and porn movie actors and actresses. The sex workers union in **France** represents about two hundred and fifty prostitutes. There are sex workers unions in Cambodia, Canada, India, the UK, and many African nations.

Real Live Girls?

Can it really be pimping if the prostitute is not human? Korean law-makers faced this question when a group of people were found to be pimping inflatable sex dolls. "Doll experience rooms" were intro-duced in around 2004 as an alternative to actual sex with an actual prostitute. The rooms, outfitted with a sex doll, bed, and computer, went for the equivalent of about $15 an hour. The dolls, referred to as "dirty wives," became such popular partners that entire hotels were converted into something resembling doll brothels. While police find the trend disturbing, they are still struggling to find a way to make it illegal.

Why Don't We Do It in the Road?

It's universally accepted in cultures around the world: No matter *who* is having sex or *how*, there's one *where* that's out of the question: in public. It's not just taboo—it's against the law. So why can't people stop having sex in elevators, libraries, public restrooms, retail store changing rooms, taxi cabs, ski lift gondolas, golf courses, public park benches, and perhaps the most legendary place of all: the bathrooms of airplanes? These are just a few of the places where people experience the joy of sex . . . if they can get away with it.

Dangerous at Any Speed

Switzerland is home to Europe's only legal sex drive-through. After escalating complaints from citizens viewing unspeakable acts in cars, officials in **Zurich** created a series of "sex boxes" behind which people can do as they wish without horrifying passersby. The boxes look like cubicles for cars with three closed sides, and they make quickie drive-through sex on the side of the road possible and semi-private.

In **New Mexico**, couples can't have sex in their cars unless there are "tightly drawn curtains" over the windows. In a certain town in **Arizona**, couples can't have sex in cars with flat tires, and the fine for the offense varies depending on whether the act takes place in the front or back seat.

In one **Tennessee** town, women are barred from "pleasuring a man" who is behind the wheel of a car.

In Harrisburg, **Pennsylvania**, it is against the law to have sex with a truck driver at a tollbooth.

In **New Jersey**, you can have sex in your car as long as you're careful not to bump into the horn while doing the act; that will result in a fine.

In a 2010 survey, 15 percent of respondents in six countries admitted to having sex while driving their cars. In fact, more said they had sex behind the wheel than doing other activities such as playing video games while driving. Having sex while driving is not always explicitly against the law, but it tends to lead to other traffic offenses such as reckless driving, crossing the median, and speeding.

In **Norway**, a man pulled over for driving 133 kilometers (about 83 miles) per hour in a 100 kph zone was slapped with a driving ban and a heavy fine after police discovered that not only was he speeding and veering in and out of lanes, but he had his girlfriend in his lap and they were "doing the act," as police said.

In one **Oklahoma** town, it is illegal to masturbate while watching two people have sex in a car.

In **England**, it's illegal to have sex on a parked motorcycle.

In **Detroit**, sex in a car is legal as long as it's parked on one's own property.

The mayor of a small town in **Alabama** was arrested for having sex in a parked car outside a Waffle House. The couple was in full view of restaurant patrons.

A **Swedish** couple charged with pubic indecency for a sex act on a bus denied the charge, claiming that the woman was merely rubbing the man's "tummy" inside his shirt.

Public displays of affection in cars are illegal in **Eboli, Italy**.

It's not illegal to have sex on the hood of a police car in **Holland**, but a man doing just that was taken to jail for insulting the officer who had politely asked him and his partner to break it up.

In **Scotland**, a couple used the hood of their own car, but had sex in the parking lot of a police station. A passerby came into the station and reported a naked man in the parking lot. The police found this to be true, and told the man to step away from the woman. The couple was apparently too consumed in the moment to respond, and the police had to intervene. The couple pleaded guilty to "breach of the peace."

Wisconsin law says that "whoever has sexual intercourse in public is guilty of a Class A misdemeanor." Couldn't get much clearer than that, which is why a Wisconsin couple was recently arrested for doing it in a public park as a crowd of up to twenty people watched.

In **Kansas**, "lewd and lascivious behavior" is a crime, and is defined in part as "engaging in sexual intercourse or sodomy with any person or animal with knowledge or reasonable anticipation that the participants are being viewed by others; or the exposure of a sex organ in a public place, or in the presence of a person who is not the spouse of the offender and who has not consented thereto, with intent to arouse or gratify the sexual desires of the offender or another."

Having sex in public would break **Texas**'s public lewdness law, but doing it in private "recklessly" while "those who might be offended or alarmed" are present is also against the law.

Do You Like Piña Coladas?

Making love at midnight in the dunes of the Cape may sound romantic, but it's actually illegal. In 2009, park officials at Cape Cod National Seashore in **Massachusetts** said that the number of citations they've issued and complaints they've received for disorderly conduct (the charge associated with public sex acts) has tripled in recent years. Having sex in the dunes is against both federal and state law, and also violates park environmental laws designed to protect the fragile ecosystem. The offense typically incurs a federal misdemeanor charge, which carries a $150 fine plus a $25 court fee for an outdoor violation. The dramatic increase in dune sex has overtaxed the park's limited ranger staff, who have had to break up large group sex acts of many varieties. A complaint was even received from a whale watch boat captain, who observed from out at sea a large group sex act happening on the beach. Rangers have also received an increase number of reports of flashing.

In **Tossa del Mar** on Spain's Costa Brava, sex on the beach is now illegal. In nearby **Benidorm**, the problem of beach sex became so widespread that local authorities closed the beach between midnight and 7 A.M. Those found breaking the law are slapped with a 750-euro fine.

For a British couple in **Dubai** found guilty of offending public decency by having sex on the beach (and being unmarried while doing so), the punishment was a bit more steep: three months in jail. The pair made international headlines for their arrest in 2008. The convicted couple maintained their innocence, saying that they had only been hugging and kissing. Observers said that the sentence was surprisingly lenient, as confinement for up to two years had been expected. The sentence was later suspended and the couple deported back to their native England.

A seventy-two-year-old man and a forty-nine-year-old woman were arrested for "outraging public decency" by having oral sex on the beach on the **Isle of Wight**.

Would You Like to Hear about Our Special?

Restaurants are private property, and as such are free to make their own rules about what can and can't happen within their confines. But one **Toronto** restaurant raised eyebrows when it offered diners a very unique Valentine's Day special: "Please feel free to have sex in our restrooms." Public health officials said it would be all right as long as the bathrooms were kept clean and no sex took place in the kitchen. The bathrooms were individual rooms with locking doors, so the sex couldn't be considered "public."

Please Keep Off the Grass

According to the British Sexual Offences Act 2003, sex in public is all right if there is a "reasonable expectation of privacy." Otherwise, you might be arrested for "outraging public decency." So where could you reasonably expect privacy? How about in front of the

Queen's window? A drunk couple was arrested for public indecency after they were found having sex on the lawns of Windsor Castle while the Queen was in residence. The Queen's guards watched and commented from upstairs windows of the castle, while groups of tourists took photos and videos. The moment finally came to a crashing halt when secret service officers told the couple to knock it off, then handed them off to the authorities.

In one area of **Amsterdam**, gay sex is legal in public parks. Local officials claimed that a law against public sex is unenforceable anyway, so why bother having a law against it?

Come Fly with Me

While some may brag about having sex that's out of this world, it's actually against the rules. According to its commander, sex is banned in the International Space Station to ensure that astronauts keep things strictly professional.

Speaking of the Mile High Club, some airline passengers hoped that the added amenity of double beds in the Singapore Airlines' A380 Airbus flights would mean that they'd finally achieve membership in that exclusive group. Unfortunately for those hopefuls, a company spokesperson confirmed that taking advantage of the extra space in order to get busy instead of get comfortable is unacceptable behavior.

But what about sex in the cockpit? It's not actually against Federal Aviation Administration rules. But one pilot lost his license when a video was release of him receiving oral sex from a porn star while flying over San Diego. The charge against him was reckless operation of the plane. The incident inspired many jokes, including, quite predictably, "that's why they call it the cockpit."

Seeing God

In 2002, a couple was charged with public indecency for having sex in St. Patrick's Cathedral in **New York City** while an announcer (who was also arrested) broadcast the incident live on the radio. The announcer, a comedian and radio program producer, provided commentary as the couple carried on just feet away from Catholic worshippers. The couple was participating in a radio show contest, which challenged listeners to have sex in the riskiest places possible in the city. Committing the act in a church merited twenty-five points, while doing it in Rockefeller Center would pull in thirty, and public sex with a firefighter or police officer would rate one hundred points. The couple and announcer were discovered by an usher, who observed a man who appeared to be urinating and a woman naked from the waist down. The usher called the police, who tuned into the broadcast on their way to the scene.

In **Italy**, a drunk couple having sex in a church confessional were given a warning for disturbing a church service and committing obscene acts.

In **Alabama**, a couple was caught and taken to jail for having sex on the altar of a Baptist church.

Passion at the Mall

In **Arizona**, a mall cop let a couple go with a warning the first time he found them having sex against the side of a pickup in the parking garage, even as the woman flipped off the security camera in the middle of the act. But when they simply moved to another floor in the garage, and then went to have drinks at a mall bar, he had had enough. The woman was charged with trespassing, public sexual indecency, indecent exposure, and incapacitation by alcohol in a public place, and the man with public sexual indecency, indecent exposure, and possession of a suspended driver's license.

Getting High

Police were called to a construction site when onlookers reported seeing what they thought was a couple having sex on a crane. The police used a public address system to demand that they come down. Since it was private property and the woman's father owned the equipment, no charges were filed.

A couple in **Sydney, Australia**, "got busy" in a centrally located clock tower in the middle of the work day as crowds gathered below. The pair disappeared before anyone could find out who they were, and local authorities asked through the media that they come forward to no avail.

Going to the Dogs

A phenomenon called "dogging," involving people meeting online and then arranging to have sex in public places, started to evolve in **Great Britain** around 2004, much to the chagrin of law enforcement officials. The phenomenon became so widespread that officials encouraged local residents to form patrols to discourage dogging in areas near schools or too close to local traffic. However, in 2008, police chiefs were encouraged to arrest participants only as a last resort, which caused public outcry because the majority of the country finds the practice to be indecent.

Checking Out More than Books at the Library

A **Connecticut** woman was arrested after leaving her children in the reading area and going to have sex with a man in a library bathroom. In addition to public indecency (for which the man was also charged), the mother was charged with neglecting her children.

Under Construction

When a **South Carolina** couple entered a home under construction with the intention to have sex there, they were arrested for second-degree burglary instead of trespassing. That's because they weren't married, and unmarried sex is still a crime in South Carolina. Their intention to have sex in the construction site became intention to commit a crime, hence the more serious charge.

Going Bananas

The leader of a **New Guinea** cult promised his followers that their banana crops would increase tenfold if they would start having sex in public. They did, and a man who left the group said that "young men and women including married couples were walking around naked and having sex in public places without being ashamed of themselves." While the roughly ten members who participated were not charged, the leader fled when he was tipped off that he would be arrested for "illegal activities."

You, Me, and Everyone We Know

You can never get enough of a good thing. If having sex with one person is great, then it stands to reason that doing it with several (or even several dozen) must be even better—right? However, there are laws about that sort of thing. In some places, group sex is strictly forbidden no matter where you do it. In others, law enforcement officials don't trouble themselves with what goes on behind closed doors. At least, as long as no one is making a profit off of it.

If It Ain't Got That Swing

Orgies are not illegal in **Canada**, said a court ruling after participants in one of **Montreal**'s roughly two dozen swingers' clubs were arrested. The court ruling said that since the sex was consensual between adults and took place in private rooms in the club, it was legit.

On the other hand, swingers' clubs are illegal in **Croatia**. The owner of the country's first clubs was arrested for "facilitating prostitution." The man argued that the country could not expect to become part of the European Union if it wasn't willing to accept swingers' clubs like the rest of modern Europe.

Singapore is known to have some of the most conservative laws in the world (oral sex is still illegal there), but swinging isn't prohibited. According to law enforcement officials, swinging is legal if it happens behind closed doors, is consensual, and no money changes hands.

Two men running a swingers' club in **Connecticut** were arrested for obscenity and public indecency, but the charges were later dropped. They were, however, liable for violations including smoking inside a public building, nudity, sex acts (covered under public indecency laws), not serving food where alcohol is served, and improper use of a service bar.

In trying to shut down a **Texas** swingers' club, officials charged the operators with suspicion of criminal activity for possessing a large amount of alcohol in their home. The club operators, who had been arrested before, were skirting prostitution laws by asking participants to make "donations" rather than charging them a fee for participating in swinging parties.

Swinging is perfectly legit in most places as long as there's no fee involved. **Thailand's** "king of the swingers," a British citizen, was arrested after he advertised his swinging birthday party and charged admission to its fifty participants. Police broke up the party and released the participants, but the swinger king was held for questioning. The offense he was charged with carries a hefty fine and/or up to ten years in prison.

In conservative **Iran**, a swingers' group was also arrested after the country's "morals police" found the group through online advertisements. Since adultery is against the law, those involved could be stoned to death if found guilty.

The Big O

Orgies are illegal in the outdoors in **England** if they take place in the presence of unconsenting onlookers. In 2007, firemen in the town of **Avon** stumbled upon an all-male orgy taking place in some bushes, and they were later fined and suspended because, instead of reporting the incident, they stayed and watched, shining their flashlights on the group (which appears to indicate that they were not *unconsenting* onlookers). They were found to have brought disrepute to their department.

A hotel restaurant manager in **Minnesota** filed an "indirect" sexual harassment suit after walking in on top hotel managers having an orgy on the tables in her restaurant. The orgy violated the company's policy of protecting employees from any behavior in which they felt threatened by or exposed to unwanted sexual content or contact.

In China, orgies are against the law according to the group licentiousness statute, which bans private gatherings where the main activity is sex. The wording of the law doesn't specify types of sex, but rather any group "participating in licentious activities in violation of social morality." The punishment ranges from up to five years in prison to short-term detention or surveillance. The law is described by some as "the last of the draconian laws of the Cultural Revolution."

A fifty-three-year-old computer science professor made news when he became the first Chinese person in two decades to be arrested for the group licentiousness law. The man operated a sex club out of his home. Eighteen participants in the club were jailed for up to two and half years for the crime, and the professor received three and a half years. Law enforcement officials say the sentence was so steep because he refused to admit to the "malicious nature" of his conduct because he pled not guilty. After the arrest, the country's leading sexologist started a nationwide campaign to have the law repealed. The sexual freedom advocate said that the law was a violation of privacy and should be abolished. But officials were not swayed, and in polls, the majority of the Chinese public still found the idea of orgies an affront to public decency.

A seventeen-year-old girl in **Dongguan, China**, was arrested for the same crime of group licentiousness. But what about the three boys she was being licentious with? No charges for them.

Orgies are absolutely against the law in ultra-conservative **Saudi Arabia**, where the only approved sexual contact happens behind closed doors between married men and their wives (of which there may be several). But the Mawadda Social and Family Reconciliation and Counseling Center in that country reported a sharp increase in the number of couples reporting participating in orgies in 2006. According to the report, the influence of the Internet created a desire for such behavior, and more and more women reported that their husbands had asked them to participate in group sex.

In **Russia**, a former psychologist turned cult leader pressured over one hundred of his followers to have "uncontrolled sexual relations with each other in the presence of minors." The man was on the run from authorities for years until he was finally found and arrested on numerous charges.

An "orgy for peace" scheduled for World Orgasm Day 2008 in **Tel Aviv, Israel**, was cancelled because the sponsoring group received threats. Scheduled to take place at a private location with consenting adults, the event would have been perfectly legal.

Sex and
the Single Gal

No sex before marriage! That message rang from the pulpits and made its way into the courts for hundreds of years. While things have loosened up considerably in many parts of the world, there are still places where sex before marriage is strictly taboo, and other places where it's not taboo, but somehow still against the law.

Fornication

Until 2006, fornication (sex outside of marriage) was illegal in **North Carolina**. The law said that "if any man and woman, not being married to each other, shall lewdly and lasciviously associate, bed, and cohabit together, they shall be guilty of a Class 2 misdemeanor."

Georgia struck down a similar law in 2003, and the **District of Columbia** did away with their anti-fornication law in 2005. **Virginia** got rid of theirs in the same year—about time for a state with the motto "Virginia Is for Lovers." In her finding repealing the law, the judge stated, "We find no principled way to conclude . . . that the Virginia statute criminalizing intercourse between unmarried persons does not improperly abridge a personal relationship that is within the liberty interest of persons to choose." No one had been prosecuted under the law since 1847. The case came to court when a man sued his girlfriend for not telling him that she had herpes.

Fornication laws still exist in **Massachusetts**, **Minnesota**, **Mississippi**, **South Carolina**, and **Utah**. In Massachusetts, "whoever commits fornication shall be punished by imprisonment for not more than three months or by a fine of not more than $30." In Mississippi, the sentence may be $500 or up to six months in prison. In South Carolina, the fine is "no less than $100 and no more than $500."

In **Minnesota**, it's illegal for single *women* to have sex. Unmarried men can do as they please. **Texas** and **Michigan** recently struck down laws making single sex illegal for both men and women. In **Rhode Island**, fornication is now legal, but until recently carried a fine of $10.

In **West Virginia**, it's illegal to falsely accuse a woman of being unchaste. According to sharia, the Islamic religious law, doing so is considered slander, and is not only illegal but also a sin.

In **Florida**, a teacher was fired from her job at a Christian school for fornication. She was engaged to be married and pregnant, but since the baby was due before the wedding, school officials decided that she did not reflect the school's values—coincidently just as she had asked for maternity leave.

In **Idaho**, fornication can get you a $300 fine and six months in jail. Some teen Idahoans have complained that law enforcement officials are using the archaic law to crack down on teen sex. A pregnant seventeen-year-old in Idaho was brought in for questioning when she applied for the state's pregnancy-related social assistance. The town's sheriff then charged her and her boyfriend with criminal fornication. The girl pleaded not guilty and received a suspended sentence, while her boyfriend pled guilty and received three years of probation, forty hours of community service, and a $10 fine.

Premarital sex in **India** became officially legal with a 2010 Supreme Court ruling.

Fornication is illegal in the following countries: **Afghanistan, Iran, Kuwait, the Maldives, Morocco, Pakistan, Qatar, Saudi Arabia, Sudan, Syria, the United Arab Emirates**, and **Yemen**.

In **Iran**, premarital sex is illegal, but the punishment for the crime differs for men and women. Females over the age of nine can receive anything from one hundred lashes to the death sentence; males are not punished until the age of sixteen, at which time they may receive thirty to forty lashes.

In **Pakistan**, the punishment for premarital sex is a prison sentence of up to five years. In Saudi Arabia, the punishment for premarital sex is flogging.

In **Afghanistan**, men and women both can be stoned to death if they are unmarried and are found to have had sex.

In a shocking 2010 case, a British woman in **Dubai** was arrested for having premarital sex after reporting having been raped.

A South African scuba diving instructor was arrested and held in the **United Arab Emirates** for having premarital sex with the boss of the diving company she worked for. The woman later received a pardon from the country's ruler when physical evidence showed that she had never actually had sex with him. In the same country, a Moroccan woman was sentenced to one hundred lashes for the same accusation.

Please State Your Name and Religion

In **Malaysia**, unmarried couples are barred from being alone in close proximity to each other in a private place, but only if they're Muslim. Hindu and Christian couples can fornicate privately to their hearts' content. In 2009, a Malaysian Muslim couple was arrested for *trying* to have sex in a car. Even though the act never took place, each was sentenced to six strokes with a cane because they were drinking alcohol, which is also illegal.

Malaysian police made headlines on Valentine's Day 2010 when they raided a hotel and arrested twenty-five couples for premarital sex, but let non-Muslim couples go. Each couple faces fines of up to $1,000 dollars and six months in prison.

Like a Virgin

Virginity is highly prized in **Egypt**, so much so that Egyptian women will use a "virginity-faking kit" if necessary to convince their husbands of their purity. The kit, which costs around $30 and is available online, is manufactured in China. It is inserted before sex, and during the act it releases a substance that looks like blood, simulating the rupture of the hymen that takes place during virginal sex. Egyptian lawmakers recently banned the kit, and an Egyptian scholar called for those found importing them to be exiled from the country or even to face the death penalty. Women do have other options, though: Doctors will perform a "hymen restoration" surgery for around $200. In some Islamic countries, families can have their daughters "certified" as virgins at an official clinic.

A rampant Internet rumor states that virgins aren't allowed to marry in **Guam** and that professional "deflowerers" roam the countryside doing their duty to prepare girls for marriage. The idea is a complete fabrication. Guamese officials traced the rumor to an issue of the French magazine *Marie Claire*, and the country boycotted the magazine and had public burnings of previous issues in barbecue pits. The country's lieutenant governor called the article "degrading and clearly written in ignorance."

A twenty-two-year-old American woman posted her virginity for sale on the online auction site eBay and received over ten thousand bids, with a winning bid of $3.7 million. Because the woman was a resident of an area in the state of **Nevada** where prostitution is legal, she was not breaking the law and her offer was considered a legitimate service for sale. The girl said she was planning to pursue graduate school and needed the money to finance her education. The official exchange of said service was arranged to take place at one of the state's legal brothels.

Let's Run Away Together

In **Fiji**, eloping is against the law in some villages.

In **India**, anyone over eighteen can get married without asking their parents, even though arranged marriages are still the norm. Couples who elope, however, are often afraid to return to their villages because they fear retribution from parents and other relatives.

In **Afghanistan**, a young couple traveling to Pakistan to be married were followed by villagers and executed before they could get to the border. According to Taliban officials, they had committed immoral acts out of wedlock.

The practice of bride kidnapping has been outlawed in the **Caucasus**, **Central Asia**, and some areas of **Africa** and **Southeast Asia**. But in reality, it is still practiced. According to the centuries-old tradition, a man goes with his friends and abducts the woman he wants to marry from her home and brings her to his family's house. Spending even one night away from home casts doubt on the woman's virginity; therefore her family may urge her to accept the marriage so that she will not bring shame on them. About one-fifth of marriages in **Uzbekistan** today are some form of bride kidnapping.

Cheaters Never Prosper

Is marital fidelity a quaint old concept or a legal obligation? It depends on where you live and your religion. While in many U.S. states adultery is merely grounds for divorce, in others it's much more.

Your Cheating Heart Can Land You in Jail

Adultery is still illegal in the following U.S. states: **Alabama, California, Colorado, Georgia, Hawaii, Idaho, Illinois, Massachusetts, Michigan, Minnesota, Mississippi, New Hampshire, New York, Oklahoma, South Carolina, Utah,** and **Wyoming**.

According to **Alabama** law, "if any man and woman live together in adultery or fornication, each of them must, on the first conviction of the offense, be fined not less than $100, and may also be imprisoned in the county jail or sentenced to hard labor for the county for not more than six months. On the second conviction for the offense, with the same person, the offender must be fined not less than $300, and may be imprisoned in the county jail, or sentenced to hard labor for the county, for not more than twelve months; and for a third or any subsequent conviction with the same person, must be imprisoned in the penitentiary or sentenced to hard labor for the county for two years."

In **California**, "sexual intercourse by a married woman with a man other than her husband [is] regarded as an offense against public morals, not merely as a breach of the obligation of marriage." No mention is made of a married *man's* obligations.

Colorado's law is pretty clear and straightforward: "Any sexual intercourse by a married person other than with that person's spouse is adultery, which is prohibited."

"Open adultery" is against the law in **Florida**, which means that if a couple has a secret affair, they can't be prosecuted. Since 2003, three people in the state have been charged with the crime. It requires proof and carries a sentence of up to two years. If a woman is found to be an adulterer, she forfeits her right to alimony.

In **Idaho**, adultery is a crime punishable by a fine of up to $1,000 and three years in prison.

In **Massachusetts**, those who commit adultery can be slapped with a fine of up to $1,000 and/or three years in jail.

In **Michigan**, **Oklahoma**, and **Wisconsin**, adultery is considered a felony. In **Michigan**, you could even be sentenced to life imprisonment for it.

In **Minnesota**, a married woman is prohibited from having sexual intercourse with a man other than her husband. The crime is a gross misdemeanor with a possible sentence of up to one year in jail or a fine of $3,000. Married men in Minnesota, it appears, can do as they please.

Mississippi's adultery law has been in place for one hundred and fifty years. A couple was arrested and jailed for the crime in 2010 when a wife reported her cheating husband. He and his mistress spent the night in jail and were released on $500 bond.

In 2010, the **New Hampshire** state legislature voted to keep a two-hundred-year-old law that bans adultery. Under the original law, adulterers were made to stand on the gallows for an hour with a noose around their necks. The punishment was later changed to a $1,200 fine. Legislators said that overturning the law would cause problems in civil divorce cases.

In 2010, a **New York** woman was charged with adultery and public lewdness after having sex with a man who was not her husband on a picnic table near a playground at a public park during daylight hours. The arresting officer knew her husband and knew that the law was still on the books in the state.

In **South Carolina**, "any man or woman who shall be guilty of the crime of adultery or fornication shall be liable to indictment and, on conviction, shall be severely punished by a fine of not less than $100 nor more than $500 or imprisonment for not less than six months nor more than one year, or by both fine and imprisonment, at the discretion of the court." This law made headlines when the state's governor admitted an affair in 2009. However, since his affair took place in Argentina, the state had no jurisdiction.

Technically, adultery isn't illegal in the U.S. military, but falls under the articles which regulate bringing disrepute to the armed services. Adultery can't be prosecuted unless proof exists in the form of a confession, photos, or video. A marine who admitted to adultery in 2009 was sentenced to ninety days in prison.

According to an 1889 law in **Puerto Rico**, if a couple divorces because of adultery, the guilty party forfeits "all that may have been given or promised him or her by the innocent one, or by any other person, in consideration for the latter." The same is true in **South Africa**.

Break Your Vows, Break the Law

In **South Korea**, adultery was a crime until 2009. **Uganda** scrapped its adultery law in the same year. In **India**, adultery is not a crime, but a social offense. In **Taiwan**, it's illegal, but is rarely enforced.

In **Malaysia**, it's still a crime for a man to "entice" a married woman away from her husband, although the law is no longer enforced.

In the **Philippines**, adultery is illegal for both men and women, and carries a minimum jail sentence of seven years. A British man and his Filipina lover were jailed after she became pregnant before her separation from her husband had become legal.

In **Swaziland**, a cheating man may be fined by forfeiting livestock to the family of the woman he has cheated on.

In **Cambodia**, the offense of adultery is punishable by up to a year in prison and a fine of between $50 and $250.

Adultery is illegal in **Fiji**, with penalties determined at the village level.

A British woman living in the **United Arab Emirates** was arrested for adultery when her husband reported her to the authorities. The couple (both from England) had been living in the country for ten years. The crime carries a one-year prison sentence.

In **Afghanistan**, **Nigeria**, and **Saudi Arabia**, stoning is still the punishment for adultery. There are legal specifications about the size of stones that should be used. Some Islamic scholars debate the clarity of the stoning law, proposing that the Qur'an states that if an adulterer asks for forgiveness, he or she may be absolved. Others insist that it is clear that stoning is the only stipulated punishment, even though the word "stoning" never appears in the scripture.

In **Iran**, only the female adulterer is stoned to death. A 2010 case of a woman who was to be stoned for adultery drew international response, with authorities around the world calling for a repeal of her sentence. The woman's stoning was put on hold, and later her sentence was commuted to lashing instead.

According to sharia law, for adultery to be convicted there must be four witnesses to the act or one or the other involved in it must confess. A married man who accuses his wife of adultery doesn't need the additional witnesses, but has to swear four times that he saw the act, and the wife must either confirm or deny the charge. If she swears four times that she didn't do it, she is supposed to be considered innocent.

In **Jordan** and **Syria**, if a man finds out that his wife has cheated and he responds by killing her or the man with whom she has cheated, he is excused from prosecution.

In one remote **Vietnamese** village, adultery is permitted one day a year, when people are allowed to cheat on their spouses with an ex-love. The event is a time-honored tradition which developed because love marriages were once uncommon and young couples in love had to end their relationships and marry the person of their parents' choosing.

A **Thai** woman and her lover were imprisoned for a year in Bahrain for adultery. The woman was married to a Bahraini man, who reported her.

In the **Maldives**, adultery is illegal and punishable by public flogging. In 2009, one hundred and fifty women and fifty men faced the punishment. In the same year, three women in Malaysia were caned for the offense.

In **China**'s Guangdong province, it's against the law to keep a mistress. Male officials who are found to have a mistress may be fired. In **Fiji**, the police department has a "zero tolerance" policy on adultery, and officers accused of it are fired immediately.

Oral Arguments

Who's to say *how* consenting people can and can't have sex? Apparently, the court of law. Of particular interest to the court is oral sex. Can it happen between a man and woman? Two men? Two women? Any combination of the above? Until recently, contact between the mouth and genitals was a subject of great concern for lawmakers in some places, and laws regulating that interaction still linger today.

Oral America

Oral sex could be considered illegal in **Georgia**, **Idaho**, **Louisiana**, **Massachusetts**, **Minnesota**, **Mississippi**, **North** and **South Carolina**, **Oklahoma**, and **Virginia** according to those states' "crimes against nature" laws, which prohibit "unnatural copulation" that includes a range of things from oral and anal sex to bestiality. The fact that the 2003 U.S. Supreme Court case Lawrence v. **Texas** (in which a gay couple was arrested for sex in their own home) ruled these laws unconstitutional doesn't mean they're not still on the books. In reality, few are ever enforced, but there are some noteworthy exceptions.

In 2007, a seventeen-year-old **Georgia** high school student got a ten-year sentence for receiving oral sex from a fifteen-year-old student at the same school. If the two had had intercourse, the maximum sentence would have been less than a year. The state legislature changed the crime to a misdemeanor, but the change didn't apply retroactively. The boy ended up serving over two years until the sentence was finally overturned as cruel and unusual punishment.

In **Kansas**, an eighteen-year-old mentally impaired boy was sentenced to seventeen years in prison for oral sex with a fourteen-year-old boy. If the sex had been with a female, his maximum sentence would have been fifteen months under the so-called Romeo and Juliet laws.

In **Maryland**, oral sex was illegal only for same-sex couples until 1990. In **Texas**, that ban is still in place, but was voided by the 2003 Lawrence v. Texas decision. In 2010, some Texas lawmakers reintroduced a law to outlaw gay sex.

Arizona overturned its oral sex ban only in 2001.

It's not illegal to have oral sex in **Michigan**, but doing it in public can get you arrested for public indecency, which one woman found out after doing so in a Michigan parking lot.

While oral sex isn't illegal in **New York City**, it's illegal to solicit it from a cop, as rap star D'Angelo discovered when he did just that in 2010.

In **Colorado**, oral sex isn't illegal, but it's considered sexual abuse if you're a prison employee doing it with an inmate. A jail secretary was jailed herself for six months when it was found that she had been having oral sex with a man she was supposed to be supervising.

One **Washington** man solicited oral sex from a prostitute, then turned her in to police for prostitution.

In **Florida**, it's illegal to force another person to have oral sex. But when a Florida man attempted to do it to his wife, she bit his penis and was arrested for assault. The man was not charged.

A **California** school district removed all copies of *Merriam-Webster's Collegiate Dictionary* from area schools because the dictionary includes a definition for oral sex. According to district officials, a student was trying to find the definition for another word and stumbled upon the objectionable phrase, described as "oral stimulation of the genitals." While the definition leaves much to the imagination, the student's parents were upset and demanded the school take action. Kids are barred access to *Merriam-Webster's* until a team of teachers reading the dictionary can decide if there are any other objectionable phrases in the book.

Oral Planet

In **Singapore**, oral sex is illegal, but officials are considering making it legal after two widely publicized cases. A woman found out her husband was cheating on her, so she performed oral sex on him, then reported it to the police to get him in trouble. And a police officer was jailed for two years after receiving oral sex from a fifteen-year-old girl. Since the officer was considered to be an otherwise law-abiding citizen, debate erupted about whether the law is fair.

A gay man in **Singapore** was arrested for having oral sex under the law which states: "Any male person who, in public or private, commits, or abets the commission of, or procures or attempts to procure the commission by any male person of, any act of gross indecency with another male person, shall be punished with imprisonment for a term which may extend to two years." The country is considering lifting the ban on heterosexuals, but leaving it in place for homosexual couples. There is also a consideration that would make oral sex legal as long as it is followed by penile-vaginal penetration.

In **Malaysia**, oral sex is considered to be a crime against nature and carries a fine of flogging and/or a jail sentence of up to twenty years.

Until recently, oral sex was legal in **Indonesia**, a country which is primarily Muslim. But in 2003 the practice was outlawed, punishable by up to twelve years in prison.

In the **UK**, oral sex is against the law for those under the age of sixteen, even if both parties consent to it. Forced oral sex specifically became part of the law under the 2003 Sex Offenses Act.

While **Islamic countries** have the most restrictive sex laws in the world, there's no law preventing oral sex between a husband and a wife as long as it's a form of foreplay and both parties cleanse properly afterward. All other types of oral sex are illegal.

Competitive Oral Sex?

While oral sex isn't against the law in **Greece**, nine British holiday-makers were arrested there for taking part in an oral sex competition on the beach. Since the women were paid to take part in the competition, it was considered prostitution.

It's also against the law to offer good grades in exchange for oral sex, as a **Florida** teacher found out when he repeatedly offered a student an A in exchange for it. He was arrested for lewd conduct.

Overexposed

They don't call them private parts for nothing: They're supposed to stay private. But some people like to show them off, and they can do a good job of calling attention to themselves. Lawmakers are kept plenty busy coming up with ways to keep them covered up.

Showing Off

On the subject of indecent exposure, the state of **Virginia** says: "Every person who intentionally makes an obscene display or exposure of his person, or the private parts thereof, in any public place, or in any place where others are present, or procures another to so expose himself, shall be guilty of a Class 1 misdemeanor."

In **California**, the law is a bit more detailed. There, indecent exposure applies to "every person who willfully and lewdly, either: 1. exposes his person, or the private parts thereof, in any public place, or in any place where there are present other persons to be offended or annoyed thereby; or, 2. procures, counsels, or assists any person so to expose himself or take part in any model artist exhibition, or to make any other exhibition of himself to public view, or the view of any number of persons, such as is offensive to decency, or is adapted to excite to vicious or lewd thoughts or acts."

In **Louisiana**, the charge for exposing yourself would be obscenity and is expressed as "exposure of the genitals, pubic hair, anus, vulva, or female breast nipples in any public place or place open to the public view with the intent of arousing sexual desire or which appeals to prurient interest or is patently offensive."

In **Canada**, "every person who, in any place, for a sexual purpose, exposes his or her genital organs to a person who is under the age of fourteen years is guilty of an offense punishable on summary conviction." The Canadian act specifies that "mere nude sunbathing is not of sufficient moral turpitude to support a charge for doing an indecent act."

In the **UK**, exposing your genitals is not per se illegal; it depends on the intent. Skinny-dipping, for example, would not be illegal, while flashing people "with the intent to alarm or arouse" would be.

Penal Code

An erection that shows through a man's clothing is illegal in **Arizona**, **Florida**, **Idaho**, **Indiana**, **Massachusetts**, **Mississippi**, **Nebraska**, **Nevada**, **New York**, **Ohio**, **Oklahoma**, **Oregon**, **South Dakota**, **Tennessee**, **Utah**, **Vermont**, **Washington D.C.**, and **Wisconsin**. In several states, that means that even if covered, a man's genitals must not be "in a discernibly turgid state." In **Mississippi**, displaying the said turgidity would result in a fine of up to $2,000. In San Mateo, **California**, to be against the law, the penis must be erect and turgid.

In **California**, a man was charged with felony indecent exposure when he put on a puppet show with his penis as the puppet. The man had wrapped string around his penis and was standing with his pants down outside of an apartment building, moving the string to make his penis move like a puppet.

No Nudes Is Good Nudes

Laws regarding nudism (as opposed to indecent exposure) vary around the world. The baseline defense of nudism is that nudism is not intended to alarm or arouse. In private clubs and on private beaches where there is no reasonable expectation that the nudes will be seen by others, nudism is generally legal in most countries.

After nudism became widespread on Queensland beaches in **Australia**, local officials decided to start enforcing a 1931 law barring public nudity.

In **Arkansas**, nudist law is particularly stringent: "You may not be nude in Arkansas in the presence of any person of the opposite sex who is not your spouse." In addition, it is "unlawful for any person, club, camp, corporation, partnership, association, or organization to advocate, demonstrate, or promote nudism, or for any person to rent, lease, or otherwise permit his land, premises, or buildings to be used for the purpose of advocating, demonstrating, or promoting nudism."

A **Colorado** woman known in her area as "the nude gardener" was threatened with eviction from her property for gardening in a thong, pasties, and gloves. The woman said that since she was covering her genitals, she wasn't breaking the law.

The tiny canton of Appenzell, **Switzerland**, has banned nude hiking. The offense had become so widespread that people from all over Europe had flocked to the area to hike in the buff. Opponents say the practice is not only immoral but also unsafe because of the dangerous exposure to UV rays that happens at high altitudes. Now those hiking in the buff will face a 200 Swiss Franc fine.

The town of Brattleboro, **Vermont**, had to institute an emergency ban on public nudity after the town's teens got in the habit of hanging out in the central parking lot in the nude, doing things like holding Hula-Hoop contests and riding bikes. When older people and even naturists from out of town started following suit, the town council decided it was time for action. After the emergency ban expired, the town council voted to permit nudity again.

In **Oregon**, it's illegal for a student-run organization to encourage its members to be "totally or substantially nude" in public.

Public nudity in laid-back Boulder, **Colorado**, became so widespread that lawmakers proposed a ban on it, which would apply to anyone older than ten who exposes any portion of his or her private parts, including the areola of a female breast.

While toplessness is common on **French beaches**, it was recently banned on the urban beach that's set up alongside the Seine each summer. Lawmakers said that urban nudity was a threat to public order. Thongs were banned in the same bill.

An **Australian** legislator introduced a ban on toplessness, which is quite common on the country's beaches.

In **Romania**, a measure was proposed to bar women over sixty from going topless because they are "ugly" and might frighten away tourists. Law enforcement officials admitted that the sight of topless seniors often made them "sick." The measure was later scrapped.

Sleepless in Seattle

In 2009 and 2010, "bikini baristas" (scantily clad coffee servers) in the **Seattle** area were involved in several incidents such as charging customers $80 to "flash their breasts, expose their crotches, lick whipped cream off their coworkers' genital areas, and pose naked for pictures." In response, city lawmakers proposed an amendment (still pending) to the Public Morals code prohibiting a person from "intentionally exposing any part of the genitals or pubic area, parts of the buttocks, the areola, nipple, or more than half of the breast area located below the top of the areola" on "streets, sidewalks, driveways, parking lots, automobiles (whether moving or not), and businesses open to the public, including those containing a drive-through window." It also bans "body paint or dye, tattoos, latex, tape, or similar substances applied to the skin to mask any of the above anatomical areas," and "substances that can be washed off the skin and those designed to stimulate the regions."

Nude but Not Nudist

A **Virginia** man was arrested for indecent exposure while standing naked in his own home. A woman and her child walked through his yard, saw him naked, and called the police. The police said they believed it was the man's intention to be seen, since he was standing in front of his window and he knew there could be passersby. The charge is punishable by up to a year in jail and $2,000 in fines.

In Villahermosa, **Mexico**, it's illegal to be nude even inside your home. The ban was set in place due to the proliferation of people in this very warm climate walking around in front of their windows au naturel. The penalty is over $100 for first-time offenders or up to thirty-six hours of jail time.

Badda Bing

Nude and topless dancing is illegal in **Missouri**, where female strip club employees must cover their breasts along a "horizontal line across the top of the areola and extending across the width of the breast." The state's law prohibits "the showing of the human male or female genitals, pubic area, vulva, anus, anal cleft, or cleavage with less than a fully opaque covering, or the showing of the female breast with less than a fully opaque covering of any part of the nipple or areola."

Strippers in **Missouri** clubs may not touch patrons. In 2010, the state legislature passed additional measures prohibiting the sale of alcohol in the clubs and banning the clubs from staying open past midnight. The state was immediately hit with lawsuits from club owners challenging the law.

Missouri law is particularly harsh on male strip club dancers, who must be at least partially covered, and can't be erect (in the sexual sense of the word) while dancing.

In some **U.S.** jurisdictions, the law requires that at strip clubs female nipples must be covered with pasties.

In **San Diego**, patrons of strip clubs must stay six feet away from dancers.

Topless dancing is legal in **North Carolina**, but dancers can't be bottomless.

Strip club laws in Houston, **Texas**, are considered to be very restrictive. Strip clubs are not to be located within one thousand feet of one another, a law aimed at eliminating the town's "strip club row." They cannot be within fifteen hundred feet of a church or day care center, and patrons in the clubs must stay at least three feet away from the dancers.

In **Ohio** strip clubs, there's a no-touch rule.

Lap dances are off the menu in **Detroit** strip clubs. However, the city council repealed a previous law that required dancers to wear pasties.

In **Atlanta**, exotic dancers must be over the age of twenty-one if alcohol is served in the club in which they work.

Hard liquor can't be sold in **Virginia** strip clubs.

In the past, it was common practice for strip clubs in **Las Vega**s to give $10–$100 bonuses to taxi drivers delivering patrons to their doors. Now the IRS is requiring that the clubs issue the taxi drivers W-9 forms to fill out for those bonuses.

An **Oregon** law which prohibited live sex shows and nude dancers was struck down as unconstitutional in a state appeals court. The court ruled that the law infringed on free expression.

Strip clubs were outlawed in **Iceland** in 2009. The country's prime minister, a woman, stated that the institutions were rife with human trafficking and wouldn't be permitted in their country, known for its strong human rights record.

In the **UK**, strip clubs aren't illegal everywhere, but it's now illegal to advertise for lap dancing and stripping positions in government employment centers. In the past, nude performances weren't outlawed per se, but nude performers weren't allowed to move. To get around that law, strip clubs created tableaux vivants, or living tableaus. A stationary nude would be surrounded by clothed dancers who would move fans around her, periodically revealing her nudity.

UK strip club laws vary by jurisdiction. In Westminster, strippers must wear g-strings, but in other parts of the city, they are not allowed to.

In the Jiangsu province of **China**, it's now illegal for exotic dancers to perform at funerals. The practice developed as a way to improve funeral attendance (the more people who attend a funeral, the better the deceased will fare in the afterlife). Dancers who were paid around $300 would dance clothed around the funeral procession, then strip to their underwear upon arrival at the cemetery. Families are now required to submit funeral plans to officials for approval within twelve hours of a death.

Exhibit A

Streaking, mooning, and flashing are all considered exhibitionist behaviors and can be against the law depending on the circumstances and jurisdiction. Streaking is illegal in the **UK**, **Canada**, and most **U.S.** jurisdictions (under the assumption that it is intended to alarm). It became so common at sporting events in the UK and the United States that sports authorities passed laws prohibiting "interrupting a sporting event," which include hefty fines and jail time.

In the **United States**, "flashing" is the expression commonly used to describe women quickly exposing their breasts or genitals and men exposing their genitals. It falls under public indecency laws, but in many cases is tolerated.

Two streaking women in **Tennessee** were arrested for indecent exposure for going door to door ringing doorbells while nude. They were also charged with public intoxication.

Not all streakers are necessarily exhibitionists. A **Tennessee** man arrested for streaking told police that he did it because he was bored and had nothing else to do.

In 2006, a **Maryland** judge ruled that mooning could be considered a form of free speech. Indecent exposure laws, he said, specify genitals and not buttocks.

On the other hand, an Irish student in **Senegal** was arrested for mooning and sentenced to a month in jail.

Lawmakers are still mulling the fate of a twenty-one-year-old who mooned a passing car in **Washington** State. He may have to register as a sex offender in the state because there was a fourteen-year-old riding in the car he mooned.

American rap star Foxy Brown was arrested for mooning another woman. The arrest came in part because Brown was in violation of a protective order the other woman already had against her. The charges against her included public lewdness, criminal contempt, menacing, and harassment.

Fashion Victims or Criminals?

Cities all over the United States, including **Chicago**, **Atlanta**, and **New Orleans**, have passed ordinances that make it illegal to wear droopy drawers which show off underwear or buttocks.

In Flint, **Michigan**, if your pants fall "below the buttocks" you could be looking at up to a $500 fine or a year in jail for disorderly conduct or indecent exposure.

After a teenager in Riviera Beach, **Florida**, was arrested and held in jail overnight for his droopy drawers in 2008, a local circuit judge ruled the town's ordinance unconstitutional.

A twenty-four-year-old man in Bainbridge, **Georgia**, was arrested for indecent exposure as his pants sagged while riding a bike.

In Yakima, **Washington**, indecent exposure laws include "cleavage of the buttocks," which includes visible thongs. The crime carries a fine of up to $1,000 or ninety days in jail. If a child under the age of fourteen is thought to be a victim of this form of indecent exposure, the perpetrator is looking at a $5,000 fine and up to a year in jail.

In Lafourche Parish, **Louisiana**, the law prohibits "any indecent exposure of any person or undergarments," or a person "dressing in a manner not becoming to his or her sex."

Keeping It in the Closet

A ttitudes about gay and lesbian sex vary widely around the world, and laws sometimes reflect those mind-sets. In some places, laws haven't quite kept up with changing attitudes, and in others they are a fairly accurate reflection of the local culture. Lawmakers often get pretty specific: Gay male sex is outlawed while female isn't; oral sex is okay, but penetration is not. Gay sex is often outlawed under laws that cover sodomy (which could be oral or anal sex, hetero or homosexual) or buggery (which includes bestiality). In other places, it is classified as "the detestable and abominable crime against nature."

Out Around the World

Seventy-six countries have some sort of restrictions on homosexuality. Male-male sex is illegal in forty countries in the world. In **Uzbekistan**, that only includes anal sex (other types are not covered in the law). In **Fiji**, men only are covered in the anti-sodomy law, which carries a five- to fourteen-year sentence.

In the **United Arab Emirates**, single men can be sentenced to up to fourteen years for gay sex, but a married man found with another man can be sentenced to death by stoning.

In **Iran**, statistics show that over four thousand gay men and lesbian women have been executed for their sexual orientation since 1979. The executions are typically either by stoning or hanging.

In the **Solomon Islands**, male-male sex is punishable by up to ten years in prison. In **Barbados**, gay sex is still illegal, although no one has been prosecuted under the law in recent memory. In **Jamaica**, it carries a sentence of up to seven years.

In **Malawi**, male-male sex is considered a crime under the country's sodomy and indecency laws. A gay couple in that country was sentenced to fourteen years in prison, but later released on humanitarian grounds after there was an international public outcry. The couple was arrested after they held a commitment ceremony at the hotel where one of them was employed. The couple is thought to have been the first openly gay couple in their country's history.

In **Senegal**, men can be sentenced to up to eight years in prison for having sex with other men.

In **Uganda**, the death penalty and life in prison were only recently dropped as sentences for being found guilty of sodomy.

In **Armenia**, it's only illegal for men to have anal sex with each other. The maximum penalty for this offense is five years in prison.

In **Nepal**, being convicted of sodomy (in any form) carries a sentence of up to life in prison.

In **Malaysia**, gay sex in which there is penetration is considered an unnatural offense and is punishable by up to twenty years in prison, a fine, and/or caning.

In **Singapore**, male-male sex carries mandatory jail time of up to two years. Lesbian acts which involve "riotous, disorderly, or indecent behavior" in a public setting are illegal, and carry either a fine not exceeding $1,000 or imprisonment not exceeding one month. However, the country has yet to bring a single case to court under this provision.

In **Zimbabwe**, it's illegal for people of the same sex to hug, kiss, or hold hands.

In **Zambia**, gay sex can get you fourteen years in prison.

In the **United States**, gay sex has often been regulated and criminalized under sodomy laws, and sometimes under fornication laws. There are only five states in which same-sex sodomy is the only type that is illegal.

The 2003 landmark U.S. Supreme Court decision in the case of Lawrence v. Texas effectively made *all* U.S. anti-sodomy laws unconstitutional. The case developed when two Texas men who were having adult consensual sex in the privacy of their own apartment were arrested under the Texas statute that stated: "A person commits an offense if he engages in deviate sexual intercourse with another individual of the same sex." The men fought their case all the way to the Supreme Court, which ruled that such a law is a violation of the fundamental right to privacy protected under the Constitution. But despite this ruling, there are still anti-sodomy laws on the books.

Virginia's sodomy law was ruled unconstitutional in 2005. It states that "if any person carnally knows in any manner any brute animal, or carnally knows any male or female person by the anus or by or with the mouth, or voluntarily submits to such carnal knowledge," he or she must pay a penalty of up to five years in prison. When Virginia was still a colony, the penalty for sodomy was death.

In **Alabama**, sodomy is still illegal for both genders, hetero- or homosexual, punishable by up to a year in prison and a $1,000 fine. In **Florida**, it's illegal for men and women of either sexual orientation, but it's a misdemeanor with a penalty of up to sixty days in prison or a $500 fine. In **Louisiana**, it's a felony with a sentence of up to five years and a $2,000 fine. In **Mississippi**, sodomy can get you up to fifteen years in prison. In **Idaho** it's a felony, with a sentence from five years to life.

In **Kansas**, only same-sex sodomy is illegal, carrying a fine of up to $1,000 and six months in prison. In **Oklahoma**, it's also same-sex only, and it's a felony with a punishment of up to ten years in prison.

While the **Montana** legislature repealed the state's anti-sodomy law in 2003, the state's Republican party moved to re-ban the practice in 2010. A group in **Arizona** lobbied to have their state's anti-sodomy law put back on the books as well, but the measure was never adopted.

Sodomy is still illegal within the **U.S. military**.

It was only in 2010 that **California** dropped its law requiring mental health agencies to research a cure for homosexuality.

Planet Pride

Fifty-three countries have some sort of law protecting gays from discrimination. In twenty-six countries, there is some sort of protection for same-sex civil unions or marriages.

Playing for Both Teams

Three bisexual softball players were banned from playing in the Gay Softball World Series for not being gay enough. Officials stated that the tournament was not the Bisexual World Series, therefore the men were not eligible to play. The players sued, but the North American Gay Amateur Athletic Alliance found that as a private organization, the Series is free to discriminate as it wishes.

I'm Too Sexy

Is it possible to look too sexy? To be too sexy when you talk, walk, read, write—or cheerlead? It depends where you are and what exactly it is you're doing. Being sexy in your own bedroom is fine as long as it's not so loud that it disturbs the neighbors. But if you are on the dance floor in Indonesia, make sure your moves aren't too sexy, or you may end up in the slammer.

A Kiss Is Just a Kiss

Kissing, holding hands, or any other public displays of affection are against the law in **Iran**.

While **India** has recently passed more progressive laws, public displays of affection are still considered taboo, at least socially. In 2009, a young married couple was arrested for kissing in public in Delhi, but was later cleared of the charge. The maximum sentence the charge carries is three months in prison. An Israeli couple who married in a public park in India was fined for kissing at their own wedding.

In **Sri Lanka**, public displays of affection such as kissing or holding hands in public are against the law. In one town, police rounded up over two hundred teens for public indecency within a two-week period. In most cases, the teens were remanded to the custody of their parents, but twenty couples were brought to court.

In **Dubai**, it's illegal to kiss or hold hands in public. Infractions may result in a prison sentence. A British couple in Dubai was arrested for kissing in a restaurant. The pair was tipsy and was also fined for drinking alcohol. Attempting to leave the country rather than serve a month in prison for the offense, they were detained and their passports taken.

In Aceh, **Indonesia**, people of the opposite sex sitting too close to each other in public can be given a warning. The province is the only place where sharia law is not an addition to the criminal code, but *is* the criminal code.

Kissing and hugging in public are against the law in Kuala Lumpur, **Malaysia**.

It's illegal to kiss on **French** trains, but there's no penalty for doing so. A similar ban at a train station in **England** was met by such an outcry that the station lifted the ban and the stationmasters established a designated kissing zone instead.

"Displays of affection not appropriate in a public setting" are off limits in several NFL (National Football League) stadiums, including **Seattle**, **St. Louis**, and **Philadelphia**.

In Pocatello, **Idaho**, there's an eighteen-minute limit on public displays of affection. In a town in **Iowa**, the limit is five minutes. In Halethorpe, **Maryland**, the limit is one second.

The mayor of Guanajuato, **Mexico**, faced such a backlash over a proposed public kissing ban that he reversed course and invited all visitors to kiss with impunity in the "kissing capital of Mexico."

The city of **Moscow** is still considering a citywide public kissing ban.

A **Singapore** cab driver was arrested for kissing the hand of a female passenger when they reached their destination. It turns out that her boyfriend was a police officer and the cabbie was charged with outraging her modesty. That charge can include anything from hugging someone without his or her permission to rape or taking offensive photos of a woman in a public place.

Keep It Down Over There

Britain's Anti-Social Behaviour Orders are designed to protect those who live in close proximity to others from the annoying habits of their neighbors, such as having sex too loudly. Two women have been arrested for this offense. According to reports, even a partially deaf neighbor was affected by one woman's boisterous lovemaking (she also pounded on the walls, which caused vibrations). Not long after her first court date, the woman was cited three additional times within ten days. While she was originally sentenced to eight weeks of jail time, the sentence was later commuted. The other woman's fiancé was banned from her apartment building and fined close to $400 for disturbing neighbors.

More than two-thirds of **New Yorkers** report hearing their neighbors having sex, but only 14 percent complain about it, and another 16 percent say they actually enjoy it.

In **South Carolina**, a man was so annoyed by his roommate's noisy sex that he stabbed him. The man was charged with assault.

Big Mouth, Big Trouble

In ultra-conservative **Saudi Arabia**, just talking about sex can get you in big trouble. A man on a Lebanese TV talk show who shared a little too much information was sentenced to a thousand lashes and five years in prison. The man, a Saudi, took viewers on a tour of his bedroom and showed off his sex toys, which were blurred for the camera. He and his friends then sat around and talked about what turns them on. (His friends were each sentenced to two years in prison and three hundred lashes.) The man said he didn't know that the show would be broadcast in his home country. His lawyer said that there is no actual law preventing men from bragging about sex, but the court said that it fell under Islamic law, which states that people shouldn't talk about engaging in immoral behavior.

Sexting

In one **Chinese province**, the first offense of sexting (sending racy text messages) comes with a five-day jail term, then it's up to thirty days for the second, and a fine plus more jail time for the third. Repeat offenders would be publicly named in the media. So how does anyone know about your sexting? The state-run mobile phone company works with the government to monitor service and determine "unhealthy" content. To be classified as unhealthy, the content must meet thirteen criteria, which are not made public. The service provider may temporarily disable the data function on a user's phone if unauthorized use is suspected.

A **Texas** man found to be repeatedly sexting an underage girl was banned from owning a cell phone by a local judge.

What Not to Wear

Miniskirts are forbidden at a **Mexican** university because the president said they provoke attacks on women. A **Ugandan** minister proposed a miniskirt ban because they "distract drivers and lead to traffic accidents." During the 2008 Olympics in **Beijing**, women were banned from wearing miniskirts in the city.

Cross-dressing is against the law in **Haddon**, **Hopatcong**, and **Dover**, **New Jersey**; **Lafourche Parish**, **Louisiana**; **Tecate**, **Mexico**; **Dubai**; and **Malaysia**. **Oakland**, **California**, removed a century-plus–old law against cross-dressing only in 2010. It was illegal in **Guyana** until the country's supreme court recently struck down the law.

Tight jeans are against the law for Muslim women in one province of **Indonesia**. Police said that pants are too provocative, and they undertook a campaign to distribute over twenty thousand long skirts to women in the area. They also banned local shops from selling tight-fitting dresses. Under the law, nearly twenty women have been taken into custody and had their jeans confiscated. The women say that it's hard to ride the motorbikes that are their only form of transportation if you're wearing a skirt. So far, all the women police have apprehended have been on motorbikes.

In **Chile**, a miniskirt ban in one region of the country in 2009 was short-lived. Protests from women around the country caused the governor to rethink his position.

In **Iran**, woman can be ticketed for wearing clothes through which their figures are too visible or for head scarves that show too much of their hair.

In **Afghanistan**, male tailors are forbidden from taking women's measurements.

In one **Malaysian province**, women can be fined up to $200 for wearing sleeveless shirts or other clothing that the police consider indecent. Lawmakers in the province say that the laws are intended to "help people practice their Muslim faith better."

A British woman wearing a bikini in a **Dubai** mall was arrested for public indecency. The charge was later dropped.

In **Lebanon**, an unenforced but still-on-the-books law bans women from wearing two-piece bathing suits on the beach.

In Paris, **France**, there is still a nineteenth-century law banning women from wearing trousers in public. Although it is never enforced, the law states that if a woman should wish to wear trousers, she must "present herself in the central police station to obtain authorization." According to the law, the only authorized use of trousers for women is while horse riding or biking.

Love Potion?

Turn On, a soda that the makers claim is a bona fide aphrodisiac, was banned in **France** and **Denmark**, but is legal in the **United States**. The warning on the can says "this drink will arouse you," but also advises that pregnant women and people with high blood pressure or diabetes shouldn't consume it.

Bathroom Politics

In **Texas**, it's illegal to knowingly entering a restroom intended for the opposite sex.

You Go, Girl!

Saudi Arabia's strict sharia law prevents a woman from being alone with any man who is not her husband. A woman journalist, walking in the park with a male colleague, was stopped by a sharia-enforcing vice police officer. Fed up with the oppression, the woman punched the police officer in the face. She faced prison time or a lashing for her action, but gained the support of many women in the country. Authorities are still considering the case.

Too Sexy for School?

Wisconsin mandates that sex education teachers teach about condoms and other forms of birth control. But a local district attorney announced that teachers using the state-mandated curriculum could be arrested for contributing to the delinquency of minors.

A **Texas** lawmaker introduced a ban on cheerleading moves that are too sexy, but the bill failed to gain enough support in the Texas house. A **Georgia** high school dance team was dissolved after there was an outcry from parents over their suggestive moves.

Piercing Is Not a Crime . . . or Is It?

A **Georgia** lawmaker introduced a bill to outlaw female genital piercing as part of a larger bill outlawing female genital mutilation. While fellow lawmakers balked at banning the practice for adult women, it's now against the law for women under eighteen. There is no equivalent law for male genital piercing at any age. In **Florida**, a woman was sentenced to a year in jail for performing a genital piercing on a thirteen-year-old girl.

Dirty Dancing

A **Wisconsin** high school banned "dirty dancing" at school functions and equipped the school gym with surveillance cameras from multiple vantage points to enforce the rule. Those found making moves such as grinding and freak dancing (simulating rear-entry sex) are subject to removal from the premises by security guards.

In **Indonesia**, "dirty dancing" is considered amoral and it is illegal. Wearing clothing that is too revealing and performing in public is said to "stir desire." According to the law, all "bodily movements [that] are deemed obscene and capable of violating public morality" are banned. Four women and two men were arrested for the crime in 2010. The penalty for the offense is up to fifteen years in prison.

International pop stars the Pussycat Dolls were fined over $2,000 by **Malaysian** police for putting on an indecent show while in the country. According to the country's law, performers must be clothed from chest to knee and not engage in any "jumping, shouting, hugging, or kissing onstage."

A **Jamaican** dance style called "daggering" was banned from dance halls because in addition to being too lewd, it's dangerous. Rumors that a woman died of a broken neck while daggering turned out to be false, but Jamaican doctor reported that men trying to recreate the moves in the bedroom have suffered from "broken" penises (actually a tear in the tissue of the erect penis).

Fast and Loose

Under **sharia law**, it's illegal to have sex during fasting (a required religious observance during several holy periods of the year). The law says that "even if the penetration is as little as the tip of the male organ," it's sex, but "if the penetration is less than the tip of the male organ, so that it cannot be said that intercourse has taken place . . . the fast does not become invalid." There is an exception for those who forget that they are fasting or are having sex in a manner that makes them feel "helpless." If that's the case, the fast is not invalid. But if the person remembers the fast during the act, he or she should immediately stop.

Is Lying for Sex a Crime?

South Korea recently struck down an old law which penalized men who make false promises of marriage to a woman in exchange for sex. Conviction of the crime carried a sentence of up to two years in prison and a fine of $4,000. The number of men convicted of the crime had decreased in recent years from over two hundred in 1981 to fewer than fifty in 2009.

A married Palestinian man was jailed for eighteen months for rape after he told a Jewish woman that he was Jewish, ostensibly to have sex with her. The man was charged with "rape by deception." Her attorney argued that his client believed that she was having sex with a single Jewish man and would not have slept with a married Palestinian. The man denied telling the woman that he was Jewish, but rather introduced himself by a nickname that is commonly used by Jewish and not Palestinian men. He admitted to lying about being married. The law under which rape by deception is prosecuted is thought to be unique to **Israel**, although there is a similar Spanish law that only applies to those under sixteen. Because of frequent cases of Internet predators lying about their age to get access to young girls, **Massachusetts** is considering a law to prohibit the use of deceit in order to access sex.

The Gift That Keeps on Giving?

In **South Dakota**, it's a misdemeanor to expose another person to a sexually transmitted disease such as syphilis, gonorrhea, or herpes.

Deliberate transmission of the HIV/AIDS virus is a crime in **Germany**, **Australia**, **New Zealand**, **Canada**, and the **UK**. In the **United States**, thirty-four states have prosecuted individuals for the crime, which is viewed as equivalent to either manslaughter, murder, attempted murder, or assault.

Shacking Up

It used to be called "living in sin," then "shacking up," and now in most Western countries it's just "living together." In some countries, it is traditionally considered immoral, although not necessarily illegal; in others, it both.

Outside the Bonds of Marriage

Living together without being married is against the law in every country that practices **sharia law**, but it is unevenly enforced. Unmarried couples visiting Islamic countries are expected to pretend to be married when staying in hotels, and hotel staff is generally not expected to ask for proof of marriage.

In **Indonesia**, cohabitation is illegal and punishable by up to two years in prison.

In the **United Arab Emirates**, police have recently started cracking down on out-of-wedlock couples, with jail time likely, although the law states that punishment of up to one hundred lashes is allowable.

The country, which is considered to be one of the most liberal of the Middle Eastern states, had for many years turned a blind eye to couples living together and even having children together without being married.

In **Malaysia**, Muslim couples who are government employees can be evicted from government-owned housing if it is discovered that they are not married. Morality police have authority to investigate Muslim civil servants, although couples who are of other faiths are not subject to the same laws and scrutiny.

Cohabitation is considered "lewd and lascivious" behavior and is illegal in **Florida**, **Michigan**, **Mississippi**, **Virginia**, and **West Virginia**. The punishment ranges from a $500 fine to a short prison sentence.

Florida's adultery and fornication law states: "If any man and woman, not being married to each other, lewdly and lasciviously associate or cohabit together, they shall be guilty of a misdemeanor of the second degree." That offense carries a penalty of up to $500 in fines and sixty days in jail. According to state records, 392 people have been arrested and charged with violating this law since 2005. The law requires proof of intercourse to sustain a conviction.

In **Michigan**, "if any persons, not married to each other, lewdly and lasciviously associate and cohabit together, or, whether married or not, be guilty of open and gross lewdness and lasciviousness, each of them shall be guilty of a Class 3 misdemeanor; and upon a repetition of the offense . . . shall be guilty of a Class 1 misdemeanor." This offense is punishable by up to a year in jail, but if the crime is kept secret for over a year, it can't be prosecuted. Judges in Michigan have denied custody or visitation rights to unmarried parents because of the law. A Michigan court of appeal declared that because unmarried couples are branded as criminals by the state's anti-cohabitation law, they would be subject to housing discrimination under laws which allow landlords to deny housing to those with criminal records.

North Carolina only recently repealed its cohabitation law, which stated that unmarried men and women couldn't even share a hotel room together. According to the law, "any man and woman found occupying the same bedroom in any hotel, public inn, or boarding-house for any immoral purpose . . . shall be guilty of a Class 2 misdemeanor." While the law was rarely prosecuted, it was used against parties in divorce proceedings, and women who lived with abusive boyfriends were denied financial assistance through state's Victim Compensation Fund because the law labeled them as criminals. In the years between 1997 and 2005 (when the law was repealed), thirty-six people were prosecuted under the law and seven were convicted. One woman was fired from her job when her employer discovered that she was unlawfully cohabitating.

Until 2007 in **North Dakota**, it was a misdemeanor for a couple who was not married to pass themselves off as a married couple. This offense, which was referred to as "false representation of marital status," was punishable by a maximum of thirty days in prison and a $1,000 fine.

In Black Jack, **Missouri**, there's a municipal statute banning three people who are not related by blood or marriage from living in the same house and allowing landlords to deny housing to those living in such a relationship. The law was enacted as a way to prevent "nontraditional families" from living in the town. An unmarried couple sued the town for violation of their civil rights when they were denied a housing permit.

In **Arizona**, a woman was denied a state job because it was discovered that she was cohabitating, which was against the law. As a result of her efforts, the law was eventually repealed in 2001.

In **Tennessee**, a "paramour clause" in the state's family law prohibits cohabitation of unmarried partners if minor children are in the home. However, the law is not strictly enforceable, and a state court of appeals has rejected claims to enforce it.

In **Colorado**, making your home available for romantic trysts for unmarried couple is illegal.

In a landmark case in 2010, **India**'s Supreme Court ruled that cohabitation was not illegal in that country.

In **Vietnam**, local people may live together outside of marriage, but it's illegal for foreigners to invite locals back to their hotel rooms.

Although living together outside of marriage is common in **Bulgaria**, the country's parliament recently struck down a law to make such an arrangement legal. Only seven members of the legislative body voted to make cohabitation legal.

While **Greece** recently moved to give unmarried couples the same legal rights as married couples, the Greek Orthodox Church condemned the move and stated that relationships outside of marriage are equal to fornication.

In **Massachusetts**, it's illegal for a previously married couple to live together after they've been divorced. The same is true in the country of **Bangladesh**.

All in the Family

Incest is universally taboo and reviled, but the boundaries of what defines it shift from culture to culture. How close is too close in a family? Can first cousins fall in love and marry? Is more than one wife too many?

Kissing Cousins

According to one historian, up to 80 percent of all marriages that have taken place in history have been between cousins.

In **North Africa**, consanguineous marriages—that is, marriage between blood relatives—is the norm. These marriages keep wealth in a family. In **Middle Eastern countries**, the ideal marriage is said to be to the father's brother's daughter.

In **Korea**, there are only around two hundred and fifty surnames used, the most common of which are Kim, Park, and Lee. These names are derived from ancient clans or bloodlines that have existed in the country for millennia, and each clan is associated with a homeland or area of the country. For many centuries, it was illegal to marry someone with the same surname and ancestral home. This law was made unconstitutional in 1997 because it violates the fundamental "right to happiness" and "right to family life" guaranteed in the Korean constitution. The constitution was amended in 2002 and the new law came into effect in 2005.

In **India**, it's illegal for Hindus to marry first cousins, and in some regions it's even illegal for someone to marry anyone from the same village. It's legal for Muslims to marry cousins (including first cousins), and the rate of cousin marriage among Muslims is close to 20 percent.

It's illegal to marry your first cousin in **China**, the **Philippines**, and **Taiwan**.

In **Canada**, **New Zealand**, and **Australia**, it's legal to marry your first cousin.

It's not illegal for first cousins to marry in the **UK**. Close to half of British citizens of Pakistani origin are married to first cousins. But a man can't marry his mother, adoptive mother, daughter, adoptive daughter, aunt, grandmother, sister, niece, son's daughter, former wife's daughter or granddaughter, father or grandfather's former wife, or former civil partner's daughter or granddaughter. Women can't marry the male equivalents of these relationships.

In the **United States**, thirty states have laws against first cousins marrying. Six states have laws prohibiting marriage between cousins once removed. In **North Carolina**, double first cousins can't marry. (Double first cousins are produced when two siblings of one family marry two siblings of another family and both have children.)

In **Arizona**, the law states: "marriage between parents and children, including grandparents and grandchildren of every degree, between brothers and sisters of the one-half as well as the whole blood, and between uncles and nieces, aunts and nephews, and between first cousins, is prohibited and void. . . . First cousins may marry if both are sixty-five years of age or older or if one or both first cousins are under sixty-five years of age, upon approval of any superior court judge in the state if proof has been presented to the judge that one of the cousins is unable to reproduce." **Utah** has a very similar law. These laws address the common concern that marriages between close relatives that produce children will result in birth defects and genetic abnormalities. Studies on this issue often prove inconclusive, with some showing that there is indeed an increase in birth defects for children born of close relatives, and others showing that the increase is not significant.

In **Illinois**, marriage between first cousins is allowed if "both parties are fifty years of age or older; or (ii) either party, at the time of application for a marriage license, presents . . . a certificate signed by a licensed physician stating that the party to the proposed marriage is permanently and irreversibly sterile."

In **Maine**, the law says that "a man may marry the daughter of his father's brother or sister or the daughter of his mother's brother or sister, and a woman may marry the son of her father's brother or sister or the son of her mother's brother or sister as long as . . . the man or woman provides the physician's certificate of genetic counseling."

In **Louisiana**, **Minnesota**, **Missouri**, **Montana**, **North Dakota**, **Oregon**, **Pennsylvania**, **Washington**, **West Virginia**, and **Wyoming**, intercourse between cousins is not considered incest. In **Arizona**, it's only considered incest if the couple is under eighteen; in **South Dakota**, only if they are over eighteen.

In **Minnesota**, cousins may marry if it is part of their "aboriginal" culture. This law protects members of the Hmong immigrant minority in Minnesota, since marrying cousins is customary in Hmong culture.

In **Brazil**, an uncle and niece may marry if they first undergo genetic testing.

Here Come the Brides

According to **sharia law**, a man may keep up to four wives as long as he treats each wife equally. Countries that respect sharia generally uphold this law, although the practice varies widely from place to place. In many countries, having more than one wife is a symbol of wealth and prestige, while in others it has come to symbolize the more rural, traditional lifestyle, and is therefore looked down upon.

The **United States** passed the Morrill Anti-Bigamy Act in 1862, making polygamy illegal in any U.S. state or territory. This act was challenged by members of the Church of Jesus Christ of Latter-day Saints in **Utah**, who practiced polygamy, but they lost their appeal. The law reads: "A person is guilty of polygamy, a felony in the third degree, if he marries or cohabits with more than one spouse at a time in purported exercise of the right of plural marriage. The offense is a continuing one until all cohabitation and 'claim' of marriage with more than one spouse terminates." The law further states that this prohibition doesn't apply to people passing through the country who are lawfully in a polygamous marriage in the country in which they reside.

Despite this law, polygamy is a continuing practice among religious fundamentalist groups, primarily those who splintered off from the Church of Jesus Christ of Latter-day Saints (Mormons), which outlawed the practice in the nineteenth century. The number of people living in polygamous families in the United States is thought to be close to ten thousand, all of whom live in under two dozen communities, generally in the southwestern United States, particularly in Utah, but also Texas, Nevada, Idaho, Colorado, Wyoming, and Montana. There are a few isolated groups in Mexico and British Columbia, Canada, who also practice polygamy. While polygamy is clearly illegal in all U.S. states, it is often tolerated or overlooked in these religious communities unless the practice involves underage girls. In a famous case in 2006, the head of a polygamous religious group was prosecuted for polygamy and rape of the underage girls to whom he was "married" (which is illegal because they were under the age of consent). The man was convicted and sentenced to ten years to life in prison.

Polygamy is illegal in all countries of the **European Union**.

South Africa recognizes polygamist marriages according to the customary laws of different ethnic groups.

Polygamy is legal but rare in **Bangladesh**, in part because there's no financial incentive to have more wives: The tax rate increases for each wife taken.

Polygamy is legal in **Cameroon**, and there is no legal limit on the number of wives a man can take.

Polygamy was outlawed in **Côte d'Ivoire** in 1964, but polygamous marriages that took place before that date are legal. The penalty for polygamy is between $80 and $800 and six months to three years in prison.

Ethiopia is the only nation in the Horn of Africa in which polygamy is illegal, but the practice still exists there. One man there was discovered to have twelve wives and a total of 78 children.

The African nation of **Gabon** is unusual in that both men and women can have more than one spouse. The only restriction is that all parties involved must decide before marriage if they intend to be exclusive or have a polygamous union. Men are allowed to later take back this pledge, but women aren't.

Around a third of all marriages in **Niger** are polygamous.

In **Egypt**, Muslim men are allowed to have up to four wives, while men of other religions can only have one. In **Iran** and **Libya**, a man must obtain written consent from his first wife before taking additional wives. In **Malaysia**, a Muslim man may have more than one wife if he can prove his ability to support the additional wives financially.

Polygamy was common in **Thailand** until it was outlawed in 1935. Up until that time there were three types of marriages: the arranged marriage with an official wife, then with a "minor wife" chosen by the man, and then with a "slave wife" who was purchased.

Polygamy is illegal in the **UK**, but if a polygamous family moves to the UK, their marriage will be recognized.

Polyandry—the practice of a woman having more than one husband—isn't very common, but still exists in a few nations, including **Tibet**. It's illegal there, but still happens in rural areas, typically when a woman marries two brothers. If she has children, it is up to her to determine which man is the father.

I Take You, and You, and You to Be My Wife

Bigamy is the practice of getting married again while still married to someone else. In the **United States**, the following law applies: "A married person is guilty of bigamy, a misdemeanor, if he contracts or purports to contract another marriage, unless at the time of the subsequent marriage, 1. the actor believes that the prior spouse is dead; or 2. the actor and the prior spouse have been living apart for five consecutive years throughout which the prior spouse was not known by the actor to be alive; or 3. a court has entered a judgment purporting to terminate or annul any prior disqualifying marriage, and the actor does not know the judgment to be invalid; or 4. the actor reasonably believes that he is legally eligible to remarry." In some jurisdictions, spouses can still be liable for bigamy even if they didn't know that they were not free to remarry.

A **Kentucky** man was brought before the court for having four wives, two of whom he married in one week. Bigamy in the state carries a maximum sentence of five years in prison.

In **South Carolina**, the bigamy law says that "any person who is married who shall marry another person shall, unless his or her husband or wife has remained continually for seven years beyond the sea or continually absented himself or herself from such person for the space of seven years together, such person not knowing his or her wife or husband to be living within that time, he or she was married before the age of consent, his or her wife or husband is under sentence of imprisonment for life." The punishment for bigamy is up to five years in prison and a fine of $500.

Bigamy is illegal in **Canada** with the notable exception of the province of Saskatchewan, where bigamy, polygamy, and polyandry are legal.

Bigamy is illegal in both **Australia** and **New Zealand**.

Separated at Birth

In what sounds like the plot of a TV drama, twins were born in the **UK** and given up for adoption to different families. They grew up and married each other, not knowing they were brother and sister. When they found out, they had their marriage annulled. A couple in **Ireland** (not twins, but siblings separated by adoption and raised without knowledge of each other) found themselves in the same situation and chose to stay married and leave the country so that they could continue their life together in a place where no one knew their story.

Two recent sibling couples, one in the **United States** and one in **Germany**, served jail time for incest for their relationships. In each case, one sibling was removed from the home in childhood and the siblings didn't meet again until they were adults. In the case of the German couple, the man was an adopted brother and not biologically related to the woman. He served two years in prison for the offense of incest.

In **Sweden**, half-siblings may legally marry.

The Love That Has No Name

Imagine the most disgusting thing you could do sexually. Now take that image and amplify it by about a million. You may then be able to get reasonably close to the kinds of things people get arrested for doing. There's no way to legislate the types of things that people come up with, so in general, offenses such as having sex with lampposts falls under the category of "disturbing the peace," "outraging public decency," or plain old "indecency." There are specific laws for such appalling acts as having sex with living animals; it's often called buggery, but it might also be animal abuse. If the animal is dead, however, that could be a whole different thing (or at least that's what lawyers argue).

The Human Touch

Paraphilia is the name for a disorder which causes people to be sexually aroused by nonnormative objects or actions. One common manifestation of this disorder is sexual arousal by nonhuman objects. While there's nothing illegal about it in private, when it happens in public it can lead to an array of broken laws.

An **Iowa** man was arrested for "an unnamed sex act" in his neighbor's yard. While police wouldn't reveal the act, they did disclose that they recovered from the man's home multiple videos of the accused having sex with traffic signs around town.

A **British** man was charged with outraging the public decency when he was seen "simulating a sex act" with a lamppost in clear view of local residents.

A **Michigan** man who was arrested for breaking and entering stores six times over a thirteen-year period was, each time, found not stealing, but having sex with a mannequin from the store's window. The man told police that he found the mannequins too tempting and couldn't resist smashing windows to get to them.

Two men, one in **England** and one in **Florida**, have a thing for trees. Each was arrested for public indecency for "humping" trees in public parks in broad daylight.

A **Virginia** man was charged with indecent exposure for "performing a sex act" with an armless child mannequin on a park bench. Witnesses saw what appeared to be two people engaged in sex on the bench, but on closer inspection, it turned out to be the man "moving up and down" on top of a mannequin. The man told police he was "just trying to have a little fun."

An **Ohio** man was arrested for felony public indecency for having sex with a picnic table on four occasions. His neighbor videotaped the incidents. While the picnic table was in the man's own backyard, the charge was a felony because his home was in close proximity to an elementary school. The man apparently used the hole in the center of the table (through which an umbrella is typically inserted) for the sex act. He was sentenced to six months in prison.

A **Florida** man was arrested for trespassing and disturbing the peace after witnesses saw him having a threesome with two rubber dolls in his car, which was parked in front of a grocery store. The witnesses said they saw the man "performing an activity" on the blow-up dolls. The man was later convicted of "corrupting the public's morals and outraging the sense of public decency."

A "lonely" **Hong Kong** man who had sex with a metal park bench had to be cut loose by police. They had to take the man, with the bench still attached, to a local hospital. The man had become stuck after his engorged penis caught in one of the bench's circular openings and could not fit back out through it.

In **England**, a security guard was found "in a compromising position" with a vacuum cleaner in a hospital staff room. When he was arrested for outraging the public decency, he claimed he was cleaning his underpants. Charges were later dropped, but the man was fired. A ninety-four-year-old man in **Arizona** was charged with pubic sexual indecency after neighbors found him in their garage having sex with their vacuum. It was later found that the man had also been accused of child molestation. Surprisingly, these two are not the only ones with a predilection for vacuum-cleaner sex: A **Michigan** man was sentenced to ninety days for public indecency when he was found having sex with a car wash vacuum cleaner.

In 2010, a **Canadian** man was arrested for indecent exposure when he was seen masturbating on top of a display vehicle at a home and garden expo. The man said that he was sexually attracted to the car's roof because it was curved like a woman's body and it felt good. Police report that the man said that only certain cars arouse him. He was arrested again later on a MINI Cooper where he proceeded to "tuck, rub, and bounce his naked genitalia" on the hood of the car. He was also found having sex with a Buick Century, and admitted that he had done so with a 1967 Chevy Camaro and a 1955 Chevy Bel Air.

In 2008, an **English** man was arrested for outraging the public decency when he was found having sex with a Volkswagen Beetle.

A man in **Scotland** was arrested for disturbing the peace after two maids walked into his hotel room and found him naked from the waist down, "moving his hips back and forth as if to simulate sex" with a bicycle. The man was placed on three years of probation.

A woman who claims to have had "a physical relationship" with a piece of fence later "married" the Eiffel Tower and changed her last name to "Eiffel." The woman has never consummated the relationship with the tower, however, so she is breaking no laws. Psychologists say she is one of only five women in the world who are objectum-sexuals, or people sexually attracted to objects. One of the others is a woman who claimed to be married to the Berlin Wall.

Interspecies Encounters

Sweden is considered one of the most sexually liberated countries in the world, and since 1944 has had no laws regarding bestiality. However, when investigative reporters discovered that there was an animal sex ring in the country, lawmakers were urged to take action to protect the animals. The country's Animal Welfare Agency registered 115 cases of bestiality between 2000 and 2005, but others projections estimated that between two and three hundred dogs and cats are being sexually assaulted in the country annually.

Sex with animals is against the law in **Australia**, **Canada**, **Denmark**, and **New Zealand**.

There are fifteen **U.S.** states where there is no specific law prohibiting bestiality. **Alaska** and **Florida** don't have anti-bestiality laws, but are considering putting them into place because of repeated incidents. Since there is no specific law, those who are found committing animal sexual abuse (such as a blind man having sex with his guide dog and a man who had sex with a goat, then killed it) can only be charged with criminal mischief. A proposed measure in Alaska would expand the state's animal cruelty law to include sexual conduct, making it punishable by up to a year in jail and a $10,000 fine. In Florida, a proposal would make sex with animals punishable by up to five years in prison.

Nebraska has a very detailed bestiality law which prohibits fellatio, cunnilingus, anal sex, or any penetration "however slight" of an animal, including "any object manipulated by the actor into the anal or genital cavities which can be reasonably construed as being for nonmedical purposes."

North Carolina specifically includes birds in its anti-bestiality statute.

In **Rhode Island**, the law states that the "detestable crime against nature with an animal" carries a sentence of no less than seven years in prison.

The **Texas** statute prohibits "contact between the offender's mouth or genitals and the anus and genitals of the animal or fowl." **Utah** includes any "vertebrate creature" in its bestiality law, which of course leaves out such things as mollusks or jellyfish. A man in **Australia** was actually charged for downloading pornography that featured sex with an octopus.

Bestiality was outlawed in **Arizona** and **Washington State** in 2006. The Washington law was spurred by the death of a man from a perforated colon after having sex with a horse and by a "bestiality farm" where a man kept horses, dogs, and mice and charged people to have sex with them.

The **South Carolina** bestiality law reads that "whoever shall commit the abominable crime of buggery, whether with mankind or with beast, shall, on conviction, be guilty of felony and shall be imprisoned in the Penitentiary for five years or shall pay a fine of not less than $500, or both, at the discretion of the court." In 2009, a South Carolina man was repeatedly arrested for this crime when he was videotaped having sex with a horse in a neighbor's barn.

In **Wisconsin**, sexual gratification with an animal is against the law. One man arrested on the charge claimed to have had sex with calves around fifty times.

A **Michigan** man who had sex with a sheep was charged under the state's sodomy law and sentenced to thirty months in prison.

A **California** man was charged with animal abuse after police (who were arresting him on drug charges) found a video of the man wearing a bra and receiving oral sex from a Labrador retriever while he massaged the dog's penis.

In the **UK**, the law prohibits penetrative sex with an animal. In one case, a woman who had lost her dog found it being "mounted" by a man dressed as a woman. For other sex acts with animals, the charge is an "outrage to public decency," which is what a seventy-one-year-old man was charged with when he was seen in public receiving oral sex from a horse. Another man was charged with the same crime for having sex with a sheep and was banned from being on farms.

In the **Netherlands**, bestiality is against the law, but can only be prosecuted if it's proven that the animal suffered emotional distress. A man accused of sex with a sheep was discharged after the prosecutor was unable to get any testimony about the sheep's emotional state.

In **Belgium**, **Germany**, and **Russia**, it's illegal to make or distribute photographic images of sex with animals, although the law doesn't specifically prohibit the sex act.

In **Lebanon**, men can have sex with animals as long as the animals are female. According to Islamic law, you can't eat a lamb after you've had sex with it.

In **Peru**, it's specifically against the law to have sex with a female alpaca.

You're Dead to Me

Perhaps the most taboo of all taboos is necrophilia: sex with a corpse. In some cultures, it's so unthinkable that there don't even have to be laws against it.

Necrophilia is a crime under the 1961 **New Zealand** Crimes Act under language governing "misconduct in respect to human remains." However, there's never been a case prosecuted in the country.

In New South Wales, **Australia**, necrophiliacs are charged with "misconduct with regard to a corpse." Under the law, any "indecent interferences" with a corpse are criminal.

Only one person has ever been convicted of **Barbados**'s law against defiling a corpse.

In the **UK**, necrophilia is outlawed under the Sexual Offences Act 2003, which bans "sexual interference with a human corpse" or "depictions of such an act which appear to be real." While prosecution is rare, one mortuary worker admitted to abusing corpses one hundred times in sixteen years.

One man in the **UK** accused of murdering a young woman and raping her corpse said that he found the girl in a pool of blood in a driveway and started to have sex with her, but didn't realize until after he was done that she was actually dead. The prosecutor responded that the man's defense was "unattractive," while the defense attorney said that his client "let his lust get the better of him." The man was convicted of murder and sentenced to life in prison.

In **Nevada**, sexual abuse of a corpse is considered a Class A felony, with punishment of up to life in prison. The state's law defines this sort of abuse as "cunnilingus, fellatio, or any intrusion, however slight, of any part of a person's body or any object manipulated or inserted by a person into the genital or anal openings of the body of another, including, without limitation, sexual intercourse in what would be its ordinary meaning if practiced upon the living."

In **Hawaii**, the crime is considered abuse of a corpse and is a misdemeanor.

A **New York** hospital worker found having sex with the corpse of a ninety-two-year-old woman was held on $400,000 bail and ordered to have psychological evaluation.

Oh, Deer

A man in **Wisconsin** tried to skirt the state's law against sex with animals by asserting that the dead deer he had sex with was not an animal, but a carcass. The defendant was charged with sexual gratification with an animal, but his lawyer asserted that "the statute does not prohibit one from having sex with a carcass." The lawyer's case worked, somewhat. His client was convicted of having sexual contact with an animal (rather than actual sex) and was put on probation.

In the same state, three men charged with having sex with a corpse were found guilty of having sex without consent. While the state doesn't have an explicit necrophilia law, the state's law does say that consent must be present, and a judge ruled that a corpse cannot give consent.

Seen and Obscene

U.S. Supreme Court Justice Potter Stewart is famous for having said that when it comes to obscenity, "I know it when I see it." That statement reveals just how hard it is for people in the same country to agree on what's obscene, never mind a global standard. That may be why obscenity laws around the world vary so wildly.

That's Obscene

In the **United States**, obscenity laws vary by jurisdiction, but at the federal level the case must pass what's now called the Miller test, evaluating the following criteria: "whether the average person, applying contemporary community standards, would find that the work, taken as a whole, appeals to the prurient interest; whether the work depicts or describes, in a patently offensive way, sexual conduct specifically defined by the applicable state law; and whether the work, taken as a whole, lacks serious literary, artistic, political, or scientific value."

Nudity is not considered obscene by the Miller test, and neither is "single male to female vaginal-only penetration that does NOT show the actual ejaculation of semen (sometimes referred to as 'soft-core' pornography) wherein the sexual act and its fulfillment (orgasm) are merely implied to happen rather than explicitly shown." Any representation of bestiality, simulated rape, urination, and defecation is considered "obscene," and pornography depicting those things is illegal in the United States.

In the **UK**, pornography is outlawed under the Obscene Publications Act 1959, which prohibits articles that "deprave and corrupt persons who are likely, having regard to all relevant circumstances, to read, see, or hear the matter contained or embodied in it."

In **Canada**, what is and isn't obscene is determined by the Canadian Criminal Code. The very vague law states that "offences tending to corrupt morals" include "written material, pictures, models (including statues), records, or any other thing whatsoever" whose main purpose is "the undue exploitation of sex, or the combination of sex and at least one of crime, horror, cruelty, or violence." Material that's considered pornographic can only be sold in adult stores or on adult websites, and can't be sold to anyone under eighteen.

Pornography is illegal in **Belarus** and **Lithuania**. However, "erotic" material falls into a different category and is sold at newsstands and even in supermarkets. In the **Ukraine**, distributing and possessing pornography is illegal except for "medical purposes."

In **Iceland**, publishing pornography is punishable by a fine and up to six months in prison. Publishing child pornography carries a sentence of up to two years in prison.

Possessing and viewing pornography is illegal in **Malta**, but the practice is still widespread.

In **Brunei**, it's illegal to produce pornography except for personal use.

In **Uganda**, a law under consideration outlaws "any action that depicts unclothed or underclothed parts of a human body, such as breasts, thighs, buttocks, or genitalia, and includes actions that depict or describe sexual intercourse or any behavior that is usually associated with sexual intercourse or sexual stimulation" in literature, film, plays, audio recording, art, and fashion.

It's illegal to produce or possess pornography in **Malaysia**, the **Philippines**, and **Turkey**.

It's illegal to sell pornography on **U.S. military bases**. It's also illegal to access it on government-owned computers.

While child pornography is illegal almost everywhere in the world, it's not in **Japan**, which is one of the world's largest producers of child pornography and the second largest consumer of it after the United States.

Sex Sells

Sex stores are legal in the **UK** as long as they prohibit minors from entering and don't display their wares in their windows.

Regulations regarding sex stores vary by jurisdiction in the **United States**. In general, they're restricted to certain areas of a town and their signage cannot display sexual content.

Until 2008, it was illegal to sell sex toys such as vibrators and dildos in **Texas** according to an obscenity law which prohibits stimulating "another's genitals with an object designed or marketed as useful primarily for that purpose." The offense was punishable by up to two years in jail. When a woman was arrested in 2004 for operating an in-home sex toy party business, the state's lawmakers reconsidered the law and it was eventually repealed.

In **Georgia**, sex devices are only legal to use with a prescription from a medical doctor. The advertisement of sex toys for sale has only recently become legal in the state.

In **Mississippi**, it's illegal to "knowingly sell, advertise, publish, or exhibit any three-dimensional devices designed or marketed as useful primarily for the stimulation of the human genitalia, also referred to as sexual devices."

In **Sweden**, dildos, vibrators, and massage oil are now available over the counter at pharmacies, although they're not displayed and customers have to ask for them.

In conservative **Bahrain**, a married woman opened a sex shop which originally sold products such as edible underwear and vibrators. But shortly after it opened, the government banned the sale of sex toys. The products are designed to "help married couples enjoy sex fully," the owner said, because unmarried sex is illegal in that country. She continues to operate her shop with products like natural supplements that promise increased sexual vigor, but with such limited wares, she fears she will go out of business.

While **sharia law** regulates morality in Islamic countries, it doesn't mean that all sexual content is banned. An online Muslim sex shop, aimed at married couples and operated out of the Netherlands, is regulated according to Islamic law. Women and men enter the shop by separate clicks and can browse through products such as lubricants and aphrodisiacs. Pornography, vibrators, and dildos are not available.

The **European Union** is considering a ban on sex toys because they contain phthalates and other toxic industrial chemicals. The lawmaker who introduced the legislation said that the chemicals contained in sex toys made in Asia can disrupt the body's hormone balance and diminish male fertility, deform baby boys' genitals, and advance puberty in girls. Because of this risk, the Danish Environmental Protection Agency issues a warning to women who are pregnant or nursing not to use dildos and to others only to use them if they are sheathed in condoms. "Normal use" is not dangerous, but use for more than an hour a day is risky, the warning says.

Sex toys aren't illegal in the **UK**, but stealing them is. A Royal Mail deliveryman who had for ten years been stealing pornographic DVDs, women's underwear, and sex toys instead of delivering them was arrested in a raid.

In **Malaysia**, selling health products such sex stimulants is illegal.

In the state of **Maryland**, it's illegal to sell condoms from vending machines, except in places where alcohol is also sold.

Hangin' on the Telephone

Many U.S. states have laws making obscene phone calls illegal. In **Massachusetts**, it's illegal to "annoy or accost a person of the opposite sex" with annoying and harassing phone calls that include lewd, wanton, or lascivious behavior.

In **Washington, DC**, an obscene phone call includes "any comment, request, suggestion, proposal, image, or other communication which is obscene or child pornography, with intent to annoy, abuse, threaten, or harass another person." The penalty is a fine and up to two years in prison.

World Wide Porn

As Internet use has grown, so have the many different ways people have used it to do really perverted things. But regulating Internet porn has proven to be more complicated than anyone could imagine.

Internet porn has been blocked in **China** since 2002. Possession of pornography is punishable by up to three years in prison, a fine of 20,000 Yuan. Large-scale pornography distributors can be executed.

Watching Internet porn can get you up to three years in prison in **Indonesia**.

In the **European Union**, the law states that anything that is illegal offline (child pornography, obscene content) is also illegal online.

In **Australia**, "content hosts are required to delete Australian hosted content from their server (Web, Usenet, FTP, etc) that is deemed 'objectionable' or 'unsuitable for minors' on receipt of a take-down notice from the government regulator, the Australian Broadcasting Authority (ABA)." Hard-core porn is illegal on mobile phones, and the government is considering blocking it from the Internet as well.

Only foreign porn sites are illegal in **Egypt**. Egyptian porn sites, which are numerous, are not regulated by law.

In **Singapore**, pornography websites with "mass impact objectionable material" are blocked.

In **Saudi Arabia**, the Internet is regulated by a government agency and there is a site blacklist. According to reports, at least one hundred sites a day are added to the list.

Porn, Going Mobile

With the advent of more features and applications for mobile phones, the question arises of how to regulate porn on wireless devises. **South Africa** is considering a law that would require all mobile phones sold in the country to be fitted with porn-blocking software. In **Malaysia**, police can make random mobile phone checks to make sure there's no porn (which is illegal in that country) on the phone.

Family Hour

In the **United States**, "whoever utters any obscene, indecent, or profane language by means of radio communication shall be fined under this title or imprisoned not more than two years, or both."

In the 1978 landmark case FCC v. Pacifica Foundation, the U.S. Supreme Court ruled that only "repetitive and frequent" use of "the seven dirty words" in a time or place when a minor could hear them would be unlawful.

In **Alabama**, you can be ticketed for having obscene bumper stickers on your car. Anything which includes "obscene language descriptive of sexual or excretory activities" is considered a Class C misdemeanor.

Rated X

Films that were deemed obscene in the **United States** used to be given a rating of X, XX, or XXX, depending on the extent of graphic sex included in the film. In 1990, that rating was replaced with NC-17, which means "no children under seventeen." NC-17 films can only be shown in certain theaters which have methods for keeping children from entering the theater, including requirement of a photo ID with proof of age.

Kinky Stuff

Kink: It's a catchall expression for sexual preferences that are outside the mainstream. While in some places they may fall under "whatever turns you on," in others they can land you in jail. And for those who get turned on by watching others without their knowledge, the law generally has a strong response.

Of Human Bondage

Consensual sex between adults is typically legal in most places. But when you get into bondage, domination, and sadomasochism, the line of what's consensual isn't always legally clear. That makes BDSM a tricky legal question.

Perhaps the most famous S and M legal case was called "Operation Spanner" in the **UK**, during which sixteen men were arrested for "assault occasioning bodily harm" even though the men involved told police that they were willing participants in the "torture" that police had seen on video. The judge in the case ruled that consent was not a valid defense for the actions. The court concluded that "a person does not have the legal ability to consent to receive an act which will cause serious bodily harm, such as extreme activities of a sadomasochistic nature." The law is now commonly interpreted to mean that activities causing marks and injuries that are more than transient are prohibited.

In **Switzerland**, ownership of "objects or demonstrations, which depict sexual acts with violent content" is punishable by law. That means S and M magazines and equipment are illegal.

In **Germany**, "a person inflicting a bodily injury on another person with that person's permission violates the law only in cases in which the deed can be considered to have violated good morals in spite of permission having been given."

In **Italy**, the criminal code leaves it up to judges to determine if a case of S and M is consensual and within the law or not.

Bondage-loving **Britons** will now be subject to fines if they're found in possession of "extreme" photos of bondage, domination, or S and M. The law, passed in 2008, makes it illegal to own such images. Bondage advocates protested the law, saying they are fine with the prohibition against images that portray certain predilections such as bestiality and necrophilia, but they see no point in banning images that depict the potential for loss of life or serious injury to genitalia. Members of CAAN (Consenting Adult Action Network) say that the law is too vague and leaves too much discretion up to judges. The law came about as the result of the murder of a woman by a man who was involved in watching and making extremely violent Internet pornography.

Bondage clubs are not illegal, but in the lawsuit-happy **United States** they're subject to the same kinds of safety lawsuits of other businesses. While one bondage club patron was bound and hanging from the ceiling, the bolt that attached her restraint came free, and she came crashing to the floor and broke her jaw. She sued.

Drop Your Cover

In Bethesda, **Maryland**, you can have fetish parties at your house as long as you don't include a cover charge to participate. Neighbors tipped off police that a man on their street was holding parties featuring bondage, discipline, dominance and submission, and sadism. Police ticketed the man for land-use violations. His infringement was running a commercial enterprise out of a residential space (he was charging $20 admission and $50 for a VIP pass). If the man waived the cover charge, police said, the parties could continue because they are within the man's constitutional rights.

An outdoor fetish "block party" in **New York** was just fine with the neighbors, even though participants paid $10 to enter. Police say they issued a parade permit for the party, which took place on West 28th Street between 10th and 11th Avenues. During the party, there were several acts of "discipline" and many participants wore genital-restraining gear. The local precinct didn't receive a single complaint.

Sex Shows

Sex shows include such things as peep shows or provocative acts on stage.

Live sexual performances are against the law in Phoenix, **Arizona**. A law in Los Angeles which banned them was thrown out after it was deemed by the State of **California** to infringe on free expression. A law banning them in Portland, **Oregon**, was later overturned for the same reason.

On Your Feet

There's not exactly a law against having a foot fetish. So when a **Georgia** man was found repeatedly approaching women at a library and claiming to be an orthopedic therapist, then smelling and kissing their feet, police knew it was wrong, but weren't quite sure how to charge the man. They came up with simple battery.

Oregon authorities charged a man with two counts of third-degree sexual assault for his "foot fetish scam." The man tricked women into trying on shoes at department stores, then fondled and kissed their feet.

A **New Hampshire** man was arrested on over a dozen charges of assault for going up to women at fitness centers, asking them for help with a move or piece of equipment, and then grabbing their feet and pressing them against his groin.

A **Wisconsin** man was charged with theft after breaking into a high school and stealing fifteen hundred shoes to satisfy his foot fetish.

Strange Desires

It's also hard to figure out how to charge someone with a fetish for slurry (another word for "manure"). Police in the **UK** charged a man with breaching the terms of his probation when he was found for a second time masturbating in a vat of manure at a neighbor's farm. The man had already been jailed and banned from the farm for the first offense.

A **Japanese** man was arrested for stealing uniforms from the locker room of a football club because he has a fetish for the smell of sweat and dirty underwear.

A forty-seven-year old man in **Connecticut** was arrested in a super-market parking lot for wearing nothing but a diaper and approaching people, asking them to change him. He was charged with disturbing the peace.

A **Minnesota** man was arrested for breaking and entering colleges, hospitals, and fitness centers in order to slash rubber fitness balls with a knife, an act which he said gave him sexual pleasure. The man also admitted to popping them with his bare hands. He was held in a psychiatric facility because it was determined that he was a "danger to society."

They Like to Watch

In most **U.S.** states, voyeurism takes place "where a reasonable person would believe that he or she could disrobe in privacy, without being concerned that his or her undressing was being photographed or filmed by another; or . . . where one may reasonably expect to be safe from casual or hostile intrusion or surveillance." There are anti-voyeurism laws in every state except **Iowa**, where voyeurs are prosecuted for invasion of privacy.

In **Rhode Island**, "a person commits a misdemeanor if he or she knowingly or recklessly enters onto another person's property and for a lascivious purpose looks into an occupied dwelling through an opening or window or exposes his or her genitals to the view of others in a manner which would cause others to be alarmed or affronted."

The federal Video Voyeurism Prevention Act of 2004 states that knowingly taking a picture of someone who is naked or partially clad without their consent is a crime, but the law only applies to federal buildings and lands and military bases. Video voyeurism is a sex crime in nine **U.S.** states.

In **New York**, a person is guilty of unlawful surveillance if he or she uses or installs a "device to surreptitiously view, broadcast, or record a person" in a bedroom, bathroom, changing room, or other specified room when the person has a reasonable expectation of privacy. Unlawful surveillance is punishable by a term of one to four years in jail. If the person disseminates images that were unlawfully obtained, he or she faces the same sentence.

In **Arizona**, "surreptitious photographing, videotaping, filming, or digitally recording" is a Class 5 felony. In **Colorado**, it's called Criminal Invasion of Privacy, and it's a misdemeanor.

In **Hawaii**, installing or using a recording device "in a private place used to record persons in a state of undress or engaged in sexual conduct" is a Class C felony. However, "knowingly trespassing on property for the purpose of subjecting another person to surreptitious surveillance for the sexual gratification of the actor" is considered sexual assault in the fourth degree.

In **Louisiana**, the video voyeurism law states: "Whoever commits the crime of video voyeurism when the observing, viewing, photographing, filming, or videotaping is of any vaginal or anal sexual intercourse, actual or simulated sexual intercourse, masturbation, any portion of the female breast below the top of the areola, or of any portion of the pubic hair, anus, cleft of the buttocks, vulva, or genitals shall be fined not more than $10,000 and be imprisoned at hard labor for not less than one year or more than five years, without benefit of parole, probation, or suspension of sentence."

In **Canada**, voyeurism was added to the criminal code as a sexual offense in 2005. It had previously only been prosecuted as "breach of the peace."

Upskirting

An increasingly common form of voyeurism is upskirting, looking up women's skirts and/or taking pictures or videos of the view. A variation on this voyeuristic practice is called downblousing. In **Ohio** and **California**, upskirting is now specifically banned, carrying a penalty of to six months in jail and a $1,000 fine.

There is no specific law against upskirting in the **UK**, but the offense may be covered by the voyeurism provision in the Sex Offenses Act 2003 or as "offending the public decency."

In **Australia**, several states have passed laws specifically banning upskirting. In **New Zealand**, it's illegal according to video surveillance laws.

Cell phones are prohibited in most bathing houses and fitness clubs in **Japan** and **Korea** as a way to curb cell phone picture voyeurism.

Upskirting had become so common in **Japanese** train stations that there are signs posted in the stations warning women to be aware. Railroad police are trained to spot upskirting photographers.

I-Phones in **Japan** have a feature that always makes a conspicuous sound when a picture is being taken so that people can't be caught unawares. The sound can't be turned off even when the phone is on silent mode.

One Is the Loneliest Number

Through the years, parents and preachers have claimed that it will make you go blind or insane. But can it get you thrown in jail? Masturbation is, pardon the pun, a very personal thing, and like other acts of sexual pleasure, it's one of those things that is best done in private. But some people can't seem to resist bringing others in on what's meant to be the most personal of moments.

Off with Their Heads?

There's a long-standing Internet rumor that masturbation is illegal in **Indonesia** and the penalty is decapitation. That's only half true. It is unlawful to masturbate according to Islamic law, which requires that one remain chaste until married, so masturbation is considered the same as adultery. But in Indonesia, being found guilty of self-love will only bring you jail time and caning, not beheading. In colonial America during the time of the Puritans, however, masturbators *were* eligible for the death penalty.

If It Pleases the Court

A judge in **Oklahoma** was disbarred after being convicted of exposing himself while hearing cases. Observers reported that the judge used a "penis pump" on the job, including during a trial about a toddler who was allegedly shaken to death. A police officer who was serving as a witness saw a "piece of plastic tubing disappear under the judge's robes." Witnesses also said they heard a whooshing sound and called the sound to the judge's attention, but he said he

didn't hear anything. The officer took photographs of the devise while the court was adjourned for lunch break. In addition, semen samples were collected from judge's robes, chair, and the nearby carpet. When finally confronted about the pump, the judge claimed the device was a joke given to him by fishing buddies, and that while he may have "absentmindedly squeezed it" while sitting behind the bench, he never used it to masturbate. He was found guilty and sentenced to four years in prison and a $40,000 fine.

A **Kansas** judge was sued by a woman who claimed that he used inappropriate language and masturbated during her divorce proceedings. The woman's husband claimed that he experienced no such incident during the same proceedings.

However disturbing the stories of the judges may be, it is not as bad as the story of a man arrested for attempted rape who received additional charges for masturbating while being interrogated about his crime.

Lonely, But Not Alone

It's a misdemeanor to masturbate in public in **South Dakota**. In **Ohio**, it's illegal to masturbate where one is likely to be seen by others.

Drive-Through Wankers

A man in **Georgia** was going through an Arby's drive-through in the nude and masturbating when he pulled up to the window to collect his order. The man pulled the same stunt at a different drive-through a few months later, this time with his pants around his ankles.

A naked man in **Ontario** ordered coffee at a drive-through and masturbated with one hand while he handed the female employee his money with the other. The employee called the police and the man was apprehended nearby for indecent exposure.

A high-speed chase in New South Wales, **Australia**, led police to find a man with his pants down and his penis enclosed in a small jar of pasta sauce. The man was arrested for indecent behavior.

Men aren't the only ones who masturbate behind the wheel. An **Ohio** woman was arrested for operating a sex toy while operating her vehicle at the same time.

Cars aren't the only vehicles that seem to arouse the passion for one's own flesh. A man was arrested for masturbating on a Southwest flight to **Denver**. According to the police report, a female passenger saw a man with his eyes closed moving his hand around his groin area, which was covered with a blanket. When the woman moved seats, the man opened his eyes and admitted that he was actually doing what she thought he was doing: "You caught me," he said. Several other airlines have reported similar violations, and one woman sued American Airlines for failing to protect her from her seatmate, who ejaculated in her hair as she slept.

Tick Inspection

A man in **Oklahoma** was arrested for indent exposure while masturbating in his car, but he told police that he was just inspecting his groin for ticks.

Up on the Roof

A Dunedin, **Florida**, man was arrested for masturbating on the roof of the Pink Panther Nightclub and Showbar at 11:30 in the morning. While no one was at the club at the time, the man was arrested for lewd and lascivious behavior, loitering, and prowling.

Lending a Helping Hand

Most types of massage are legal in most places, but it depends on which part of the anatomy is being massaged. Massage of distinctly private parts (called erotic massage or giving a client a "happy ending") is considered an illegal sex service according to laws in many areas, and a massage parlor offering such services may then be classified as a brothel. Police in the **United States** have been cracking down on illegal massage parlors and in some cases have reported interrupting the "happy ending" to make an arrest.

A licensed massage therapist in **Georgia** was arrested for "masturbation for hire" when she offered a hand job to an undercover cop who had come to her for a legal massage service. The law in Georgia says that "a person, including a masseur or masseuse, commits the offense of masturbation for hire when he/she erotically stimulates the genital organs of another, whether resulting in orgasm or not, by manual or other bodily contact exclusive of sexual intercourse or by instrumental manipulation for money or the substantial equivalent thereof."

It's Lonely in the Big House

Eight male prison inmates in **Florida** were convicted of indecent exposure for masturbating alone in their jail cells. In what was described as a sting operation by a female prison guard, the men were caught in compromising positions, and since their cells are a "limited access public place," they were found guilty. The guard said that the men made no effort to conceal what they were doing and that most male inmates hide themselves under blankets while they pleasure themselves.

Hard and Fast

Under **sharia law**, masturbating during a proscribed fast voids the fast. If semen involuntarily comes from the body, it's not void, and if a man wakes from sleep to find that he's ejaculating, that also doesn't count.

Youthful Indiscretions

Teens are notorious for their overactive libidos. While they may not be able to control their own sex drives, there are plenty of laws in place to try to do it for them.

Consenting Adults

In almost every country in the world, sex is considered legal if it happens privately between two consenting adults (or in some cases two consenting, married, heterosexual adults). But who is considered a consenting adult? The youngest age of consent is twelve, in the African nation of **Tonga**. The oldest is twenty, in **Tunisia**.

In **Saudi Arabia**, there is no specific age of consent, because sex outside of marriage is illegal. But in 2009, Saudi courts denied a marriage annulment to an eight-year-old girl whose father had wed her to a fifty-eight-year-old man, saying they can't get divorced until she reaches puberty. In the same country, a ten-year-old girl who was married to an eighty-year-old man went into hiding after the wedding, but was discovered at the home of her aunt and turned over to her husband. Although the country's human rights society lodged a complaint, there is no law in place to prevent such a marriage.

Australian authorities stopped a fourteen-year-old girl from leaving the country after they discovered that her father was sending her to the family's native country of **Macedonia** to be married to a seventeen-year-old boy she had never met.

In some countries, there are different ages of consent for girls and boys, and for heterosexual and homosexual sex.

In the **UK**, "sexual touching" is illegal for those under the age of sixteen. That includes sex with "any part of the body," "with anything else," and "through anything," and could include "where a person rubs up against someone's private parts through the person's clothes for sexual gratification." While the law appears to be sweeping, officials say it's not meant to punish those under sixteen, but to protect them from abusers, including other young teens.

Teen kissing (under the age of sixteen) is against the law in **South Africa**.

Wherefore Art Thou, Romeo?

In the **United States**, the age of consent varies from state to state. Having sex with someone under the age of consent is considered statutory rape (because the party in question is too young to consent). But in certain states, the law takes into consideration the age difference between the two participants under what are called Romeo and Juliet laws, named for the most famous underage lovers in the English language. Romeo and Juliet laws allow the court to overturn a conviction of statutory rape if the offender is within three years of the victim and has no previous sex offenses. It also allows those previously convicted of such a crime to have their sex offender registration expunged. In a famous case, a Florida man was convicted as an eighteen-year-old for having sex with his fifteen-year-old girlfriend (they had started a sexual relationship when he was seventeen and the girl's mother reported him when he turned eighteen). His name was removed from the sex offender registry under the new law ten years after his conviction.

An off-duty police officer in San Jose, **California**, went to the home of his daughter's boyfriend and arrested the fifteen-year-old for having sex with his fourteen-year-old daughter. But it actually isn't a crime, and the police officer was suspended from the department for false arrest.

In **Indiana**, teens having sex can't be convicted if they can prove they are in a "dating relationship."

In some cases, those arrested for non-consensual sex have made the case that the underage person lied about his or her age. In **Ireland**, for example, the Supreme Court ruled that the country's law be amended to allow those accused to enter the defense that they had reason to assume that the underage partner was actually of age.

Does Your Mother Know?

The age of consent in **Mississippi** is sixteen. Parents are required by law to report it to the police if they know their children are having sex according to a clause in the state's law which bans "the intentional toleration of a parent or caretaker of the child's sexual involvement with any other person."

A Fine Mess

In 2001, the king of **Swaziland** completely banned young girls from having sex as a way to curb the country's AIDS crisis. Girls were told to wear woolen tassels as a sign of their chastity. If a man propositioned a girl, she was supposed to throw her tassel at his house, and the man would have to pay a fine. The ban was unsuccessful and unpopular, and the king fined himself a cow after he took a seventeen-year-old girl as his ninth wife. This action sparked protests, and over thirty thousand women gathered to burn their tassels in the country's soccer stadium.

Sextual Feelings

In the '50s, it was racy rock 'n' roll dancing. In the '60s, it was free love. Sexting is the new teen sex issue that has today's parents up in arms. Sexting is the practice of sending suggestive, nude, and sometimes downright pornographic pictures through mobile devices.

The **Vermont** legislature took up a law that would loosen the harshest consequences of child pornography for those who are between the ages of thirteen and eighteen. Teens would not be charged as sex offenders for sending pornographic images of themselves (or receiving them from others), but rather would be charged with lewd and lascivious conduct and with disseminating indecent materials to a minor (both of which carry lighter sentences).

In **Ohio**, producing, sending, or possessing child pornography is a felony. But lawmakers recently proposed that if the crime is committed by someone under eighteen, it would be classified as a misdemeanor. In 2009, a fifteen-year-old Ohio girl who sent pornographic pictures of herself to classmates agreed to a plea deal which decreased her sentence to a curfew, supervised Internet usage, and the forfeit of her cell phone.

Pennsylvania child pornography laws prohibit the manufacture, dissemination, and possession of pornographic images of children (anyone under eighteen). But in 2009, dozens of Pennsylvania teens were arrested for child pornography for taking and sending pornographic pictures of themselves. The charges for those offenses require jail time and registration as a sex offender. The state's prosecutor suggested that the guilty teens take a five-week after school course on sexual harassment. The teens refused to take the deal, insisting that they were innocent. As of press time, the case is still being appealed.

In 2010, **Louisiana** passed a law banning anyone under seventeen from sexting. Offenses carry a sentence of mandatory counseling.

Arizona passed a similar law banning minors from possessing or distributing sexually explicit images of themselves or other minors.

A girl in **Pennsylvania** was arrested on an obscenity charge when she accidentally sexed a nude, suggestive picture of herself to the wrong number. The recipient of the text turned the image over to the police.

In the **UK** and **Australia**, teens who sext are currently only given a warning.

In **Canada**, an adult sexting a teen can get a prison sentence of a year or more, but the only teens to be charged for sexting each other have been prosecuted under the relatively minor charge of "corrupting the morals" of a minor.

Sex Laws through History

Attitudes toward sex have shifted through the ages. Things that were once common are now thought appalling and vice versa. Looking back through time, it's easy to imagine that current day standards will shift again with time.

"Sinful" Babylon

The Greek historian Herodotus wrote with distain about "sacred prostitutes" in the Mesopotamian kingdom of Babylon who lived in the temples of certain goddesses and received money in exchange for sex. He was shocked that this practice was in no way associated with shame. Once they reached womanhood, Babylonian women were expected to go to the temple of the goddess Ishtar and wait until a man threw a piece of silver in her lap. The woman then would be required to have sex with the man, because saying no would be a sin. Afterward, she would return to her hometown. Once married, women were expected to be faithful and the punishment for adultery was drowning.

Ancient Greece

On the other hand, modern day people don't always regard the ancient Greeks' views of sex as particularly enlightened: Age and consent were not considered to be strong factors in who could have sex with whom. Male-male sex between boys and older men was routine, although the boys were not forced (older men courted them). Sex between younger girls and older women was also common. While much is made of "Greek love" (which is a term sometimes used to describe male-male sex, particularly anal sex), male sex between men and boys in ancient Greece was typically intercrural (between the thighs) and penetrative sex between men wasn't common. The purpose of marriage was procreation. Prostitution was legal, and both men and women took prostitutes, although it was considered unseemly for a man to have sex with another man over the age of twenty.

Ancient Rome

In Rome, who you could or couldn't have sex with depended mostly on your gender and class. For example, if an upper-class woman cheated on her husband, he was required to divorce her and take her dowry money. She wasn't allowed to remarry and could be banished or, in certain circumstances, killed by her husband. An unmarried upper-class girl found having sex could be killed (along with her lover) by her father. Or he could just banish her to an island. No one really cared what lower-class women did, and adultery wasn't a crime for men.

It was illegal for patricians to marry commoners, adulteresses, former prostitutes, anyone who had been accused of a crime, actresses, or anyone whose parents had been actors.

Seduction of a virgin or a respectable widow was a crime, punishable by forfeit of one's estate for an upper-class person or banishment for a lower-class person.

In Roman Egypt, marriage between brothers and sisters was common for about three hundred years.

Men were allowed to have sex with male slaves or female prostitutes as long as they were the "active" party in the act. Penetration of a male slave was considered a punishment for the slave. Male-male sex among freeborn men was illegal.

Men were permitted to have a concubine, but not at the same time as they had wives.

Prostitution was legal, but prostitutes had no rights.

The Middle Ages

In medieval **Europe**, celibacy was considered the ideal state because it allowed one to be closer to God. Church law was the prevailing code, so priests dictated the penance as punishments for various infractions. Handbooks of penance from the time state: "Whoever fornicates with an effeminate male or with another man or with an animal must fast for ten years. If he defiles himself (masturbates), he is to abstain from meat for four days. If a woman touches herself in the same way, i.e. in emulation of fornication, she must repent for one year. Whoever ejaculates seed into the mouth, that is the worst evil," and that person must repent until death.

In medieval **England**, the age of consent was twelve for girls and fourteen for boys. Premarital sex was not necessarily illegal, but women could be fined for having a baby out of wedlock. Prostitution was legal and even condoned by the church for a time as a necessary evil which would prevent men from committing other sinful acts. Brothels were legal, but women couldn't own them. Prostitutes were required to live in red-light districts and would be publicly humiliated if they were found outside of those areas. Men found guilty of frequenting prostitutes would have their beards shaved and were forced to stand on the pillory. Adultery and fornication in some cases were punishable by death.

Sodomy was a sin and included the following acts: solitary masturbation, mutual masturbation, copulation between the thighs, copulation "in the rear" (anal sex), male or female homosexuality (in other words, everything but vaginal sex). The crime of sodomy could be punished by mutilation, burning at the stake, hanging, or, if a priest was the guilty one, being hung in a cage and starved.

Early U.S. History

The **Puritans** were especially harsh on what they considered immorality. Kissing in public (even one's wife or husband) could get you put in the stocks for several hours.

Masturbation, fornication, adultery, sodomy, and buggery (which was defined as sex with animals) were against the law. The punishment for buggery was hanging—only one man is known to have been executed for it (a teenage boy who was found with a horse). Sodomy (which was defined as male-male sex) would also get you hanged, and "inclination toward sodomy" would get you whipped. In over one hundred years in New England, however, only two men were ever hanged for sodomy.

In the more liberal, tolerant, Quaker colony of **Pennsylvania**, the penalty for sodomy was only six months in prison. But when the Quakers relinquished control of the colony, it was changed to castration and life imprisonment for the first offense, with optional flogging every three months during the first year of imprisonment and divorce if the offender was married.

Sex between two women was outlawed in the **New Haven** colony in 1654, but no one was ever prosecuted under the law.

Fornication was punished with whipping, banishment, time in the stocks, being burned in the face with a hot iron, or the wearing of a scarlet letter, as made famous in Nathaniel Hawthorne's book of the same name.

In 1777, Thomas Jefferson proposed repealing the death penalty for sodomy and replacing it with castration for men and boring a hole through the nose of a woman. But his proposal was rejected and Virginia's death penalty was retained.

Intermarriage between races (called "miscegenation") was outlawed in 1664 in **Maryland**, but specifically applied to slaves and indentured servants. In 1691, it became illegal for free people of different races to intermarry. People who had parents of different races were called mulatto and were not allowed to marry European Americans. In the **Louisiana** territory, marriage between whites and people of color was against the law, but cohabitation and sex were not and were common. After the Revolutionary War, all prior miscegenation laws were abolished and citizens of the United States were free to marry regardless of race (although new miscegenation laws were introduced later).

Fellatio was outlawed in **Connecticut** in 1821, and at the same time the penalty for sodomy was reduced from death to life in prison. The last known death sentence for sodomy was carried out in 1801 in **California**, which was then under Spanish rule. An eighteen-year-old boy was shot by a firing squad for the offense.

Victorian and Pre-Victorian Era

In seventeenth-century **England**, brothels were regulated by the Disorderly Houses Act of 1751. Apparently, it was common to deny being the keeper of such a house, because the act stated: "Who shall be deemed the keeper of such bawdy-houses, and whereas, by reason of the many subtle and crafty contrivances of persons keeping bawdy-houses, or other disorderly houses, it is difficult to prove who is the real owner or keeper thereof . . . any person who shall at any time hereafter appear, act, or behave him or herself as master or mistress, or as the person having the care, government, or management of any bawdy-house, or other disorderly house, shall be deemed and taken to be the keeper thereof, and shall be liable to be prosecuted and punished as such, notwithstanding he or she shall not in fact be the real owner or keeper thereof."

By the Victorian era, the English parliament found it necessary to create an act which read: "For the better preventing the heinous Offense of procuring the defiling of women, which certain infamous Persons do most wickedly practice," such persons "shall, being duly convicted, suffer imprisonment for a term not exceeding Two years with hard labour." The act was later amended in the Offences against the Person Act of 1861, which covered such things as assault and murder, but also sexual conduct. The act prohibited "procuring, by false pretenses, false representations, or other fraud, a girl under twenty-one to have illicit carnal connexion with any man." To clarify, "the expression 'illicit carnal connexion' means extramarital sexual intercourse." Under this law, the age of consent was twelve. Having "unlawful carnal knowledge" of a girl under ten was a felony, and it was a misdemeanor do to so with a girl between ten and twelve.

During this era, a woman in **England** could not legally refuse sex with her husband, because to do so would be grounds for divorce. Homosexuality was against the law, as Oscar Wilde found out when he was sentenced to two years in prison for the crime.

In the Victorian era, men in **Connecticut** could be arrested for pulling up a woman's dress according to a law which said that "every person who shall be guilty of lascivious carriage and behaviour, and shall be thereof duly convicted, shall be punished by fine, not exceeding $10, or by imprisonment in a common gaol, not exceeding two months, or by fine and imprisonment, or both, at the discretion of the court. . . . Lascivious carriage may consist not only in mutual acts of wanton and indecent familiarity between persons of different sexes, but in wanton and indecent actions against the will, and without the consent of one of them, as if a man should forcibly attempt to pull up the clothes of a woman." The law was repealed in 1971.

In nineteenth-century **Russia**, prostitution was legal, but prostitutes had to submit to weekly health exams and were given different passports than other citizens.

With the Criminal Law Amendment Act 1885 in **England**, the death penalty was removed for buggery and switched to "penal servitude for life or for any term not less than ten years."

The Twentieth Century

The state of **Delaware** joined the twentieth century, so to speak, in 1905 when it outlawed time in the pillory for conviction of sodomy.

Prostitution was legal in most U.S. states at the turn of the twentieth century, and was outlawed only at the outbreak of World War I. Around this same time, laws were enacted in several states for the sterilization of "sexual perverts," including child molesters and homosexuals. **California** enacted a law against cunnilingus and fellatio, but later changed the law to read "oral copulation." In **Oklahoma**, laws were introduced that criminalized sodomy for married couples and later included cunnilingus as a crime against nature.

Between 1913 and 1940, thirty-one of forty U.S. states had laws against interracial marriage. In 1913, a congressman from **Georgia** proposed a nationwide ban, calling the practice "repulsive and averse to every sentiment of pure American spirit. It is abhorrent and repugnant" and "subversive of social peace." While the bill didn't pass, many states did enact their own legislation. Many of those laws stayed in place until 1967, when they were struck down by the U.S. Supreme Court.

In 1913, **Massachusetts** had signed into law a provision that couples who couldn't legally marry in their home states couldn't marry in Massachusetts, either. This law was only repealed in 2009 in the wake of the state's passage of a gay marriage bill. Opponents of gay marriage wanted to use the provision to prevent gay couples from other states which did not allow their marriage from being married in Massachusetts.

In 1955, **Alaska** enacted the first U.S. law banning the sale of comic books that portray "sexually indecent subject matter such as adultery, homosexuality, sadism, masochism, or other perversions."

It wasn't until 1957 that an **Ohio** court ruled that a married couple had a constitutional right to have oral or anal sex.

Lesbians in **Georgia** got a break in 1963 when women were excluded from the state's sodomy law.

Until the 1970s, it was illegal for a person to walk into the hotel room of someone of the opposite sex in **Indiana**. The penalty was $25 and up to thirty days in prison.

In **Kansas**, a man could get hard labor for luring an unmarried woman into sex until the 1970s.

In 2004, **Rhode Island** repealed its 109-year-old law which made oral sex a crime for everyone, including married men and women. Oral and anal sex were illegal in Washington, DC, until 2005.

In 2010, the city council of Charleston, **West Virginia**, voted unanimously to repeal the city's ban on adultery and out-of-wedlock sex, both of which were punishable by a thirty-day jail sentence and a fine of $500.

Voluntary surgical castration is still practiced for repeat male sex offenders in the **Czech Republic**. Close to one hundred men have undergone the procedure (which removes the testicles) since it was introduced. In several U.S. states, "temporary" chemical castration (which reduces the libido) is the penalty for some sex crimes.

The Future

On the sex law horizon, there are many questions to be answered: How can cybersex be policed? How can law be effectively enforced across the Internet? There are even questions of having virtual sex in virtual online worlds (a Japanese woman was arrested for harassment in real life after she "killed" her online husband in a virtual world). Twenty-first–century lawmakers will stay just as busy as their predecessors in the past as they attempt to navigate the tricky minefield that is human sexual behavior.

Index